SRI VISHNU SAHASRANAMA STOTRAM

Mrs. Payel Chakravarty BTech (IT), MTech (IT),IIMA Certified

TABLE OF CONTENTS

PREFACE

What if just chanting a thousand divine names could bring peace, clarity, and protection into your life—no matter your age, beliefs, or background? In a world of unending noise, rapid distractions, and spiritual disconnection, the *Sri Vishnu Sahasranama Stotram* stands as a timeless beacon — calling out with the same potency and purity as it did five thousand years ago, when it was first revealed on the battlefield of Kurukshetra. It is not merely a list of divine names; it is a living bridge between the soul and the Supreme, a spiritual knowledge that has survived centuries of change, still relevant, still miraculous.

This book has not been written as a scholar's exposition, nor merely as a devotional translation. It is a heartfelt offering — an invitation to return to the sacred rhythm of your own being. In my own life, this chant has been both anchor and wings: grounding me through grief and uncertainty, and lifting me into clarity, inner peace, and strength. I believe it can do the same for you — no matter your age, background, or spiritual beliefs.

The chapters in this book are arranged with great care. We begin with **Invocation**, the traditional verses that prepare the mind and heart for divine recitation. Then comes the full text of the **Sri Vishnu Sahasranama Stotram**, in transliterated Sanskrit with meaning, allowing you to chant with understanding and devotion. **Phalashruti**, the section of benefits, is not hyperbole — countless individuals, from kings to monks to everyday seekers, have experienced these blessings in tangible ways.

To support you further, I've included a **Pronunciation Guide**, so that even newcomers to Sanskrit can chant confidently. We'll explore the **Historical Significance** of the Stotram, tracing its roots to the Mahabharata and the wisdom of Bhishma. We'll delve into the **Scientific Benefits of Chanting**, exploring how sound vibrations influence the brain and body, as confirmed by modern neuroscience and ancient yogic traditions alike.

To make this sacred text come alive, I've shared **Stories & Anecdotes** from saints, sages, and ordinary devotees whose lives were touched by these thousand names. We also explore **Regional Variations & Traditions**, showing how this one chant has been embraced uniquely across India, from Kerala temples to Himalayan ashrams.

Recognizing that chanting is more than recitation, you'll find chapters on **Meditation & Visualization Techniques**, how to set up a **Daily Chanting** routine that's practical and powerful, and tips on **How to Memorize Vishnu Sahasranama** with joy and ease.

This is not a book to be read once and shelved. It is meant to become part of your breath, your mornings, your silence, your celebrations — a companion for life.

If this ancient chant calls to you, answer. Even if you don't understand every name at first, your soul will. Begin. Chant. Learn. Let the thousand names of Vishnu awaken a thousand blessings within.

With folded hands and an open heart,
Mrs. Payel Chakravarty
(*Author, Devotee, Fellow Seeker*)

INTRODUCTION

In a world filled with relentless noise, shifting values, and inner turbulence, there comes a time when the soul yearns for something eternal — something unshakable, pure, and divinely aligned. That calling has echoed through time for over 5,000 years, carried by the sacred chant of **Sri Vishnu Sahasranama Stotram** — the thousand names of Lord Vishnu, the preserver of all that is good, just, and eternal.

This book is a humble offering and a sacred companion for seekers, beginners, and advanced spiritual practitioners alike. Whether you were drawn here by curiosity, divine guidance, or a deep yearning for peace, your presence is no coincidence. The wisdom you're about to access has transformed the lives of saints, kings, warriors, and ordinary people — providing divine protection, inner strength, and unshakable clarity across centuries.

The **Sri Vishnu Sahasranama** is not merely a string of beautiful Sanskrit syllables — it is **a living vibration**, a sacred frequency that realigns your mind, body, and spirit with the highest truth. It was first revealed in the Mahabharata, during a profound dialogue between the dying warrior Bhishma and the wise Yudhishthira. In those final moments of his earthly life, Bhishma imparted what he considered the ultimate wisdom: the 1000 divine names of Lord Vishnu — a hymn that unlocks both worldly success and spiritual liberation (*moksha*).

In today's fast-paced digital age, such sacred knowledge risks being buried under the noise. This book bridges the ancient with the modern — offering not only the full Stotram with meaning and pronunciation guidance, but also timeless insights into its **spiritual significance**, **scientific relevance**, and **practical application**.

You'll explore:

- The **origin and hidden power** of each name
- The **science behind sound and mantra**
- Inspiring **stories of miracles and divine intervention**

- Powerful **daily practices** that fit into your busy lifestyle
- Tools to **memorize the Stotram easily** — even for those with no prior Sanskrit knowledge

This book is not meant to be read and shelved — it is meant to be practiced, felt, and lived.

Whether you chant one name or all thousand, what matters most is the **bhava** — the devotion with which you approach it. You don't need perfection. You need presence.

Let this be your personal invitation to reclaim the lost art of **sacred chanting**, to invite the divine into your daily life, and to rediscover the unshakable peace that lies within you.

The divine is waiting — not in some distant heaven — but in every syllable of this chant.

Welcome to your sacred journey.
OM NAMO NARAYANAYA.

CHAPTER 1. INVOCATION

Every sacred journey begins with a step inward. Before the thousand names of Lord Vishnu are chanted, the wise seers of ancient India composed a set of verses to prepare the mind, heart, and soul. These are not mere formalities — they are like gently knocking on the door of the divine before entering its presence.

This chapter contains the **invocatory verses** traditionally recited before the Vishnu Sahasranama. They are meant to:

- **Purify the inner and outer space** around the chanter,
- **Remove obstacles** through the grace of Lord Ganesha and other deities,
- **Honor the lineage of sages**, especially Vedavyasa, the compiler of the Mahabharata, and
- **Awaken the divine presence** of Vishnu within the heart of the devotee.

These verses are timeless keys passed down for millennia, opening the door to a deeper state of awareness and receptivity.

As you begin this sacred chant, let these opening mantras become your **inner tuning fork**. Whether you are seeking peace, protection, healing, or higher understanding — this is where your connection begins.

Let us now step into the sacred syllables, verse by verse.

Verse 1

śuklāṁbaradharaṁ viṣṇuṁ śaśivarṇaṁ caturbhujam, prasannavadanaṁ dhyāyet sarvavighnopaśāntaye.

Meaning:
Let us meditate on Lord Vishnu, clothed in white, moon-hued, four-armed, and with a joyful face, to remove all obstacles.

Verse 2

yasya dviradavaktrādyāḥ pāriṣadyāḥ paraḥ śatam, vighnaṁ nighnanti satataṁ viṣvaksenaṁ tamāśraye.

Meaning:
I take refuge in Vishvaksena (another name for Ganesha), whose many elephant-faced attendants constantly remove all obstacles.

Verse 3

vyāsaṁ vasiṣṭhanaptāraṁ śakteḥ pautram akalmaṣam, parāśarātmajaṁ vande śukatātaṁ taponidhim.

Meaning:
I bow to Vyasa, the great-grandson of Vasishta, grandson of Shakti, son of Parashara, father of Shuka, and a treasure of penance.

Verse 4

vyāsāya viṣṇurūpāya vyāsarūpāya viṣṇave, namo vai brahmanidhaye vāsiṣṭhāya namo namaḥ.

Meaning:
Salutations to Vyasa, who is the form of Vishnu, and to Vishnu, who is in the form of Vyasa — the sage of Vasishta's lineage and the treasure of Vedic knowledge.

Verse 5

avikārāya śuddhāya nityāya paramātmane, sadaikarūparūpāya viṣṇave sarvajiṣṇave.

Meaning:
I bow to Vishnu — pure, changeless, eternal, the supreme soul, ever of one essence, and victorious over all.

Verse 6

yasya smaraṇamātreṇa janmasaṁsārabandhanāt, vimucyate namastasmai viṣṇave prabhaviṣṇave.

Meaning:
Salutations to the all-powerful Vishnu, by whose mere remembrance one is freed from the bondage of birth and worldly life.

Verse 7

oṁ namo viṣṇave prabhaviṣṇave. śrī vaiśaṁpāyana uvāca: śrutvā dharmānaśeṣeṇa pāvanāni ca sarvaśaḥ, yudhiṣṭhiraḥ śāṁtanavaṁ punarevābhyabhyāṣata.

Meaning:
Om, obeisance to Vishnu, the supreme one. Vaiśampāyana said: After hearing all sacred dharmas, Yudhiṣṭhira again asked Bhishma.

Verse 8

śrī yudhiṣṭhira uvāca: kimekaṁ daivataṁ loke kiṁ vāpyekaṁ parāyaṇam,

stuvantaḥ kaṁ kamarcantaḥ prāpnuyurmānavāḥ śubham.

Meaning:
Yudhiṣṭhira asked: Who is the supreme deity? What is the ultimate goal? Who should be praised and worshipped for human well-being?

Verse 9

kō dharmaḥ sarvadharmāṇāṁ bhavataḥ paramō mataḥ, kiṁ japanmucyate

janturjanmasaṁsārabandhanāt.

Meaning:
Which is the highest Dharma among all? By chanting what can a being be freed from the cycle of birth and death?

Verse 10

śrī bhīṣma uvāca: jagatprabhuṁ devadevam anaṁtaṁ puruṣottamam,

stuvannāmasahasreṇa puruṣaḥ satatotthitaḥ.

Meaning:
Bhishma replied: One who always praises the Lord of the universe, the God of gods, the infinite supreme being, with a thousand names, is uplifted.

Verse 11

tameva cārcayannityaṁ bhaktyā puruṣamavyayam, dhyāyan stuvannamasyanśca yajamānas tameva ca.

Meaning:
Worship Him always with devotion, meditate on the imperishable one, praise and bow to Him — such is the true worshipper.

Verse 12

anādinidhanaṁ viṣṇuṁ sarvalokamaheśvaram, lokādhyakṣaṁ stuvannityaṁ sarvaduḥkhātigo bhavet.

Meaning:
By constantly praising the eternal Vishnu, Lord of all worlds and overseer of the universe, one becomes free from all suffering.

Verse 13

brahmaṇyaṁ sarvadharmajñaṁ lōkānāṁ kīrtivardhanam, lōkanāthaṁ mahadbhūtaṁ sarvabhūtabhavōdbhavam.

Meaning:
He is the knower of all dharmas, upholder of Vedic traditions, enhancer of world-fame, Lord of the universe, and the origin of all beings.

Verse 14

eṣa me sarvadharmāṇāṁ dharmōdhikatamo mataḥ, yadbhaktyā puṇḍarīkākṣaṁ stavair arcennaraḥ sadā.

Meaning:
I consider this the highest Dharma: always worshiping the lotus-eyed Lord with devotion and hymns.

Verse 15

paramaṁ yō mahattejaḥ paramaṁ yō mahattapaḥ, paramaṁ yō mahadbrahma paramaṁ yaḥ parāyaṇam.

Meaning:
He is the supreme light, the supreme penance, the supreme Brahman, and the highest refuge.

Verse 16

pavitrāṇāṁ pavitraṁ yō maṅgalānāṁ ca maṅgalam, daivataṁ daivatānāṁ ca bhūtānāṁ yo'vyayaḥ pitā.

Meaning:
He is the holiest of the holy, the most auspicious among the auspicious, God among gods, and the eternal father of all beings.

Verse 17

yataḥ sarvāṇi bhūtāni bhavanti ādi yugāgame, yasminś ca pralayaṁ yānti punareva yugakṣaye.

Meaning:
From Him all beings arise at the start of creation and dissolve into Him again at the end of each age.

Verse 18

tasya lōkapradhānasya jagannāthasya bhūpate, viṣṇōrnāmasahasraṁ me śruṇu pāpabhayāpaham.

Meaning:
O King, hear from me the thousand names of Vishnu, Lord of the universe, which dispel sin and fear.

Verse 19

yāni nāmāni gauṇāni vikhyātāni mahātmanaḥ, ṛṣibhiḥ parigītāni tāni vakṣyāmi bhūtaye.

Meaning:
I will now tell you the glorious, well-known names of the great soul, sung by sages, for the benefit of all beings.

Verse 20

ṛṣir nāmnāṁ sahasrasya vedavyāsaḥ mahāmuniḥ, chando anuṣṭup tathā devo bhagavān devakīsutaḥ.

Meaning:
The sage of the thousand names is Vedavyasa, the great seer. The meter is Anushtup, and the deity is Lord Krishna, son of Devaki.

Verse 21

amṛtāṁśūdbhavo bījaṁ śaktir devakinandanaḥ, trisāmā hṛdayaṁ tasya śāntyarthe viniyujyate.

Meaning:
The seed is the moon-born, the power is the son of Devaki, the heart is the Lord praised in the Sama hymns — all for the purpose of peace.

Verse 22

viṣṇuṁ jiṣṇuṁ mahāviṣṇuṁ prabhaviṣṇuṁ maheśvaram, anekarūpa daityāntaṁ namāmi puruṣottamam.

Meaning:
I bow to Vishnu — the victorious, the great Vishnu, the powerful, the supreme Lord, of many forms, destroyer of demons, the Supreme Being.

CHAPTER 2. SRI VISHNU SAHASRANAMA STOTRAM

Benefits:

Chanting the *Vishnu Sahasranama* daily brings immense spiritual, mental, and material benefits. It purifies the mind, removes fear, and grants peace, clarity, and strength. Devotees experience protection from negativity, relief from suffering, and freedom from sins. Regular recitation fosters devotion, improves memory and focus, brings prosperity and good health, and ultimately leads to inner transformation and liberation. It aligns one's life with dharma (righteousness) and invites divine grace into every aspect of existence.

"viśvaṁ viṣṇurvaṣaṭkārō bhūtabhavyabhavatprabhuḥ,

bhūtakṛdbhūtabhṛdbhāvō bhūtātmā bhūtabhāvanaḥ. (1)"

1. Viśvaṁ: The all or the Universe.
2. Viṣṇuḥ: He who pervades everything.
3. Vaṣaṭkāraḥ: For whom the sacrificial versus are uttered in the yajnas.
4. Bhūta-bhavya-bhavat-prabhuḥ: The one who is the master and beyond the past, present and the future.
5. Bhūtakṛd: The creator and destroyer of all existences in the universe.
6. Būtabhṛd: One who supports or sustains or governs the universe.
7. Bhāvaḥ: Pure existence.
8. Bhūtātmā: The essence of all beings.
9. Bhūta-bhāvanaḥ: He who originates and develops all Elements.

pūtātmā paramātmā ca muktānāṁ paramā gatiḥ,

avyayaḥ puruṣaḥ sākṣī kṣetrajñōkṣara eva ca. (2)

10. Pūtātmā: One whose nature is purity/who is purity.
11. Paramātmā: He who is the supreme one and the Atman.
12. Muktānāṁ paramā gatiḥ: The highest goal of the liberated ones.
13. Avyayaḥ: One for whom there is no decay.
14. Puruṣaḥ: One who abides in the body or pura.
15. Sākṣī: One who witnesses everything.
16. Kṣetrajñaḥ: The knower of the field or body.
17. Akṣara: He who is without destruction.

yōgō yōgavidāṁ netā pradhānapuruṣeśvaraḥ,

nārasiṁhavapuḥ śrīmān keśavaḥ puruṣōttamaḥ. (3)

18. Yogaḥ: One attainable through Yoga.
19. Yogavidāṁ netā: The master of those who are established in the above-mentioned Yoga.
20. Pradhāna-puruṣeśvaraḥ: The master of pradhana or Prakriti and Purusha or Jiva.
21. Nārasiṁha-vapuḥ: One in whom the bodies of a man and a

lion are combined.

22. Śrimān: One on whose chest the goddess Shri always dwells.

23. Keśavaḥ: One whose Kesa or locks are beautiful.

24. Puruṣottamaḥ: The greatest among all Purushas.

sarvaḥ śarvaḥ śivaḥ sthāṇurbhūtādirnidhiravyayaḥ, saṁbhavō bhāvanō bhartā prabhavaḥ prabhurīśvaraḥ. (4)

25. Sarvaḥ: The omniscient source of all existence.

26. Śarvaḥ: Destroyer.

27. Śivaḥ: One pure.

28. Sthāṇur: One who is steady, immovable and changeless.

29. Bhūtādiḥ: Source of all elements or existing things.

30. Nidhir-avyayaḥ: The changeless and indestructible Being in whom the whole universe becomes merged and remains in seminal condition at the time of Pralaya or cosmic dissolution.

31. Sambhavaḥ: One born out of His own will as incarnation.

32. Bhāvanaḥ: One who generates the fruits or Karmas of all Jivas for them to enjoy.

33. Bhartā: One who supports the universe as its substratum.

34. Prabhavaḥ: One from whom all the great elements have their birth. Or one who has glorious births as incarnations.

35. Prabhuḥ: One who is an adept in all rites.

36. Iśvaraḥ: One who has unlimited lordliness or power over all things.

svayaṁbhūḥ śaṁbhurādityaḥ puṣkarākṣō mahāsvanaḥ, anādinidhanō dhātā vidhātā dhāturuttamaḥ. (5)

37. Svayambhūḥ: One who exists by Himself, uncaused by any other.
38. Śaṁbhuḥ: One who bestows happiness on devotees.
39. Ādityaḥ: The golden-hued person in the sun's orb.
40. Puṣkarākṣaḥ: One who has eyes resembling the petals of Pushkara or lotus.
41. Mahāsvanaḥ: One from whom comes the great sound – the Veda.
42. Anāndi-nidhanaḥ: The one existence that has neither birth nor death.
43. Dhātā: One who is the support of the universe.
44. Vidhātā: He who generates Karmas and their fruits.
45. Dhāturuttamaḥ: The ultimate support of everything.

aprameyō hṛṣīkeśaḥ padmanābho'maraprabhuḥ, viśvakarmā manusvtaṣṭā sthaviṣṭhaḥ sthaviro dhruvaḥ. (6)

46. Aprameyaḥ: One who is not measurable or understandable by any of the accepted means of knowledge-like sense, perception, inference etc.

47. Hṛṣīkeśaḥ: The master of the senses or He under whose control the senses subsist.

48. Padmanābhaḥ: He in whose navel (nabhi) the lotus (padma), the source of the universe, stands.

49. Amara-prabhuḥ: The master of Amaras or the deathless ones, i.e. the Devas.

50. Viśvakarmā: He whose Karma (work) has resulted in all that exists (Vishvam) or He whose power of creation is unique and wonderful.

51. Manuḥ: He who thinks.

52. Tvaṣṭā: He who makes all beings shrunken (Tanukarana) at the time of cosmic dissolution.

53. Sthaviṣṭaḥ: He who excels in everything in bulk or substantiality.

54. Sthaviraḥ-dhruvaḥ: Eternal One, being the most ancient. It is taken as a single phrase, the name along with its qualification.

śāśvataḥ kṛṣṇō lōhitākṣaḥ pratardanaḥ,

prabhūtastrikakubdhāma pavitraṁ maṁgalaṁ param. (7)

55. Agrāhyaḥ: One who cannot be grasped by the organs or knowledge or conceived by the mind.
56. Śāśvataḥ: One who exists at all times.
57. Kṛṣṇaḥ: The existence-Knowledge-Bliss.
58. Lohitākṣaḥ: One whose eyes are tinged red.
59. Pratardanaḥ: Destroyer of all at the time of cosmic dissolution.
60. Prabhūtaḥ: Great because of unique qualities like omnipotence, omniscience etc.
61. Tri-kakub-dhāma: He who is the support (dharma) of the three regions above, below and in the middle.
62. Pavitraṁ: That which purifies everything.
63. Maṅgalaṁ param: Supremely auspicious.

Īśānaḥ prāṇadaḥ prāṇō jyeṣṭhaḥ śreṣṭhaḥ prajāpatiḥ, hiraṇyagarbhō bhūgarbhō mādhavō madhusūdanaḥ. (8)

64. Īśānaḥ: He who controls and regulates everything.

65. Prāṇadaḥ: One who bestows or activates the Prana, the vital energy.

66. Prāṇaḥ: The Supreme Being.

67. Jyeṣṭhaḥ: The eldest of all; for there is nothing before Him.

68. Śreṣṭhaḥ: One deserving the highest praise.

69. Prajāpatiḥ: The master of all living beings, because He is Ishvara.

70. Hiraṇyagarbhaḥ: One who is Atman of even Brahma the creator.

71. Bhūgarbhaḥ: One who has got the world within Himself.

72. Mādhavaḥ: The Consort of Ma or Mahalakshmi or one who is fit to be known through Madhu-Vidya.

73. Madhusūdanaḥ: The destroyer of the demon Madhu.

Īśvarō vikramī dhanvī medhāvī vikramaḥ kramaḥ,

anuttamō durādharṣaḥ kṛtajñaḥ kṛtirātmavān. (9)

74. Īśvaraḥ: The Omnipotent Being.

75. Vikramī: The courageous One.

76. Dhanvī: One armed with bow.

77. Medhāvī: He who has great intelligence capable of grasping all texts.

78. Vikramaḥ: He who crosses (Karmana) i.e. transcends samsara. Or one who has Vih, bird i.e. Garuda as His mount.

79. Kramaḥ: Vishnu is called Kramah, because He is the cause of Kramana or crossing of the ocean of samsara by devotees, or because from Him all Krama or manifestation of the universe, has taken place.

80. Anuttamaḥ: He than whom there is none greater.

81. Durādharṣaḥ: One whom none (Asuras) can overcome.

82. Kṛtajñaḥ: One who knows everything about what has been done (Kruta) by Jivas. Also one who is pleased even with those who offer such simple offerings as leaves, flowers, fruits and water.

83. Kṛtiḥ: The word means what is achieved through all human efforts or works.

84. Ātmavān: One established in his own greatness i.e. requiring no other support than Himself.

sureśaḥ śaraṇaṁ śarma viśvaretāḥ prajābhavaḥ,

ahaḥ saṁvatsarō vyālaḥ pratyayassarvadarśanaḥ. (10)

85. Sureśaḥ: The lord of the Suras or Devas. It can also mean the greatest of those who bestow good.

86. Śaraṇaṁ: One who removes the sorrows of those in distress.

87. Śarma: One who is of the nature of supreme bliss.

88. Viśvaretāḥ: The seed of the universe.

89. Prajābhavaḥ: He from whom all beings have originated.

90. Ahaḥ: Luminous one.

91. Saṁvasaraḥ: As Time is a form of Vishnu, He is called Samvasara or a year.

92. Vyālaḥ: Being ungraspable like a serpent, He is called Vyalah.

93. Pratyayaḥ: One who is of the nature of Pratiti or Prajna (consciousness).

94. Sarva-darśanaḥ: One with eyes everywhere. As the Lord has assumed all forms, the eye-sight of all beings is His.

ajaḥ sarveśvaraḥ siddhaḥ siddhiḥ sarvādiracyutaḥ, vṛṣākapirameyātmā sarvayōgaviniḥsṛtaḥ. (11)

95. Ajah: One who has no birth.

96. Sarveśvaraḥ: The Lord of all Lords or the supreme Lord.

97. Siddhaḥ: One ever established in one's own nature.

98. Siddhiḥ: One who is of the nature of Consciousness in all.

99. Sarvādiḥ: One who is the first cause of all elements.

100. Achyutaḥ: One who never lost and will never lose his inherent nature and powers.

101. Vṛṣākapiḥ: One who shwers all objects of desire.

102. Ameyātmā: One whose form or nature cannot be measured and determined.

103. Sarvayoga-viniḥsṛutaḥ: One who stands aside completely from all bondage.

vasurvasumanāḥ satyaḥ samātmā sammitaḥ samaḥ,

amōghaḥ puṇḍarīkākṣō vṛṣakarmā vṛṣākṛtiḥ. (12)

104. Vasuḥ: One in whom all beings dwell and one who dwells in all beings.

105. Vasumanāḥ: The term Vasu means wealth or riches. Here it indicates greatness. So, it means one possessed of a great mind i.e. a mind free from attachments, anger and other evil qualities.

106. Satyaḥ: One whose nature is Truth.

107. Samātmā: One whose mind is Sama, without partiality or anger and thus the same towards all beings.

108. Sammitaḥ: This name and the previous (samatma) occurring

together, can be split in two ways – as samātmā + sammitaḥ and as samātmā + asammitaḥ.

109. Samaḥ: One unpertubed at all times.

110. Amoghaḥ: One whose worship will never go in vain, but will bear ample fruits.

111. Puṇḍarīkākṣaḥ: One who has pervaded, i.e. is realized in, the lotus of the heart. Or one whose eyes resemble the petals of a lotus.

112. Vṛṣakarmā: One whose actions are according to Vrushas i.e. Dharma.

113. Vṛṣāakṛtiḥ: One who takes form for the sake of Vrushas or Dharma.

rudrō bahuśirā babhrurviśvayōniḥ śuciśravāḥ, amṛtaḥ śāśvataḥ

sthāṇurvarārōhō mahātapāḥ. (13)

114. Rudraḥ: One who makes all beings cry at the time of cosmic dissolution.

115. Bahuśirāḥ: One with innumerable heads.

116. Babhruḥ: One who governs the world.

117. Viśvayoniḥ: One who is the cause of the world.

118. Śuciśravāḥ: One whose names and glories are very holy and purifying to be heard.

119. Amṛtaḥ: One who is deathless.

120. Śāśvata-sthāṇuḥ: One who is both eternal and firmly established, unchanging.

121. Varārohaḥ: He whose lap gives the highest blessings.

122. Mahātapāḥ: The austerity connected with creation, which is

of the nature of knowledge is of great potency.

sarvagaḥ sarvavidbhānurviṣvaksenō janārdanaḥ, vedō vedavidavyaṅgō vedāṅgō vedavit kaviḥ. (14)

123. Sarvagaḥ: One who pervades everything, being of the nature of their material cause.

124. Sarvavid-bhānuḥ: One who is omniscient and illumines everything.

125. Viṣvakśenaḥ: He before whom all Asura armies get scattered.

126. Janārdanaḥ: One who inflicts suffering on evil men.

127. Vedaḥ: He who is of the form of the Veda.

128. Vedavid: One who knows the Veda and its meaning.

129. Avyaṅgaḥ: One who is self-fulfilled by knowledge and other great attributes and is free from every defect.

130. Vedāṅgaḥ: He to whom the Vedas stand as organs.

131. Vedavit: One who knows all the Vedas.

132. Kaviḥ: One who sees everything.

lōkādhyakṣaḥ surādhyakṣō dharmādhyakṣaḥ kṛtākṛta:

caturātmā caturvyūhaścaturdaṁṣṭraścaturbhujaḥ. (15)

133. Lokādhyakṣaḥ: He who witnesses the whole universe.

134. Surākādhyakṣaḥ: One who is the overlord of the protecting Divinities of all regions.

135. Dharmādhyakṣaḥ: One who directly sees the merits (Dharma) and demerits (Adharma) of beings by bestwing their due rewards on all beings.

136. Kṛtākṛtaḥ: One who is an effect in the form of the worlds and also a non-effect as their cause.

137. Caturātmā: One who for the sake of creation, sustentation and dissolution assumes forms.

138. Chaturvyūhaḥ: One who adopts a fourfold manifestation.

139. Chatur-daṁṣṭraḥ: One with four fangs in His Incarnation as Nisimha.

140. Chatur-bhujaḥ: One with four arms.

bhrājiṣṇurbhōjanaṁ bhōktā sahiṣṇurjagadādijaḥ, anaghō vijayō jetā viśvayōniḥ punarvasuḥ. (16)

141. Bhrājiṣṇuḥ: One who is pure luminosity.

142. Bhojanam: Prakruti or Maya is called Bhojanam or what is enjoyed by the Lord.

143. Bhoktā: As he, purusha, enjoys the prakruti, He is called the enjoyer or Bhokta.

144. Sahiṣṇuḥ: As He suppresses Asuras like Kiranyaksha, He is Sahishnu.

145. Jagadādhijaḥ: One who manifested as Hiranyagarbha by Himself at the beginning of creation.

146. Anaghaḥ: The sinless one.

147. Vijayaḥ: One who has mastery over the whole universe by virtue of his six special excellences like omnipotence, omniscience etc. known as Bhagas.

148. Jetā: One who is naturally victorious over beings, i.e. superior to all beings.

149. Viśvayoniḥ: The source of the universe.

150. Punarvasuḥ: One who dwells again and again in the bodies as the Jivas.

upendrō vāmanaḥ prāṁśuramōghaḥ śucirūrjitaḥ. atīndraḥ saṅgrahaḥ

sargō dhṛtātmā niyamō yama. (17)

151. Upendraḥ: One born as the younger brother of Indra.

152. Vāmanaḥ: One who, in the form of Vamana (dwarf), went begging to Bali.

153. Prāṁśuḥ: One of great height.

154. Amoghaḥ: One whose acts do not go in vain.

155. Śuchiḥ: One who purifies those who adore and praise Him.

156. Ūrjitaḥ: One of infinite strength.

157. Atīndraḥ: It signifies "One who transcends Indra", meaning

Lord Vishnu is beyond all celestial rulers, including Indra. It highlights Vishnu's supreme authority over all divine beings and cosmic forces.

158. Saṅgrahaḥ: One who is of the subtle form of the universe to be created.

159. Sargaḥ: The creator of Himself

160. Dhṛtātmā: One who is ever in His inherent form or nature, without the transformation involved in birth and death.

161. Niyamaḥ: One who appoints His creatures in particular stations.

162. Yamaḥ: One who regulates all, remaining within them.

vedyō vaidyaḥ sadāyōgī vīrahā mādhavō madhuḥ, atīndriyō mahāmāyō mahōtsāhō mahābalaḥ. (18)

163. Vedyaḥ: One who has to be known by those who aspire for Mokshas.

164. Vaidhyaḥ: One who knows all Vidyas or branches of knowledge.

165. Sadāyogī: One who is ever experienceable, being ever existent.

166. Vīrahā: One who destroys heroic Asuras for the protection of Dharma.

167. Mādhavaḥ: One who is the Lord or Master of Ma or knowledge.

168. Madhuḥ: Honey, because the Lord gives joy, just like honey.

169. Atīndriyaḥ: One who is not knowable by the senses.

170. Mahāmāyaḥ: One who can cause illusion even over other great illusionists.

171. Mahotsāhaḥ: One who is ever busy in the work of creation, sustentation and dissolution.

172. Mahābalaḥ: The strongest among all who have strength.

mahābuddhirmahāvīryō mahāśaktirmahādyutiḥ,

anirdeśyavapuḥ śrīmānameyātmā mahādridhṛk. (19)

173. Mahābuddiḥ: The wisest among the wise.

174. Mahāvīryaḥ: The most powerful one, because Ignorance which is the cause of Samsara is His great power.

175. Mahāśaktiḥ: One with great resources of strength and skill.

176. Mahādyutiḥ: One who is intensely brilliant both within and without.

177. Anirdeśya-vapuḥ: One who cannot be indicated to another as: 'He is this', because He cannot be objectively known.

178. Śrīmān: One endowed with greatness of every kind.

179. Ameyātmā: The Spirit with intelligence that cannot be measured by anyone.

180. Mahādridhṛk: One who held up the great mountain 'Mandara' at the time of the churning of the Milk Ocean and also Govardhana in his Krishna incarnation.

maheṣvāsō mahībhartā śrīnivāsaḥ satāṁ gatiḥ,

aniruddhaḥ surānandō gōvindō gōvidāṁ patiḥ. (20)

181. Maheṣvāsaḥ: One equipped with the great bow.
182. Mahībhartā: signifies "The One Who Supports and Protects the Earth." It highlights Vishnu's role as the cosmic preserver, ensuring balance and harmony in the world.
183. Śrīnivāsaḥ: One on whose chest the Goddess Shri, eternal in nature, dwells.
184. Satāṁgatiḥ: One who bestows the highest destiny attainable, to all holy men.
185. Aniruddhaḥ: One who has never been obstructed by anyone or anything from manifesting in various forms.
186. Surānandaḥ: One who bestows joy on all divinities.
187. Govindaḥ: It signifies "The One Who Protects the Cows and the Earth." It highlights Vishnu's role as the divine caretaker, ensuring the well-being of all living beings and maintaining cosmic balance. This name is deeply associated with Lord Krishna, an incarnation of Vishnu, who is often called Govinda for his love and protection of cows and devotees.
188. Govidāṁ patiḥ: Gau means words. One who knows them is Govid. He who is the master of words is indicated by this name.

marīcirdamanō haṁsaḥ suparṇō bhujagōttamaḥ, hiraṇyanābhaḥ sutapāḥ

padmanābhaḥ prajāpati (21)

189. Marīciḥ: The supreme power and impressiveness seen in

persons endowed with such qualities.

190. Damanaḥ: One who in the form of Yama inflicts punishments on those who tread the path of unrighteousness.

191. Haṁsaḥ: One who removes the fear of Samsara from those who practise the sense of identity with Him.

192. Suparṇaḥ: One who has two wings in the shape of Dharma and Adharma.

193. Bhujagottamaḥ: One who is the greatest among those who move on Bhujas or arms, that is, serpents. The great serpents like Ananta and Vasuki are the powers of Vishnu, so he has come to have this name.

194. Hiraṇyanābhaḥ: From whose golden navel arose the lord of creation Brahmā.

195. Sutapāḥ: One who performs rigorous austerities at Badarikashrama as Nara and Narayana.

196. Padmanābhaḥ: One whose navel is beautifully shaped like lotus.

197. Prajāpatiḥ: The father of all beings, who are His children.

amṛtyuḥ sarvadṛk siṁhaḥ sandhātā sandhimān sthiraḥ, ajō durmarṣaṇaḥ śāstā viśrutātmā surārihā. (22)

198. Amṛtyuḥ: One who is without death or its cause.

199. Sarvadṛk: One who sees the Karmas of all Jivas through His inherent wisdom.

200. Simhaḥ: One who does Himsa or destruction.

201. Sandhātā: One who unites the Jivas with the fruits of their actions.

202. Sandhimān: One who is Himself the enjoyer of the fruits of actions.

203. Sthiraḥ: One who is always of the same nature.

204. Ajaḥ: The term Ajaḥ translates to "Unborn" or "Ever-Existing," highlighting that Vishnu is beyond the cycle of birth and death, unaffected by the limitations of time and creation. Unlike mortal beings who undergo birth, decay, and rebirth, Vishnu remains unchanging, formless, and timeless, existing before the universe came into being and continuing beyond its dissolution. This name reinforces his supreme transcendence, affirming that he is the eternal origin of existence, sustaining and guiding the cosmos while remaining untouched by material transformations. It embodies his divine permanence, making Ajaḥ one of the most profound affirmations of Vishnu's unbounded and unchanging cosmic presence.

205. Durmarṣaṇaḥ: It represents the undefeatable and unchallengeable nature of Lord Vishnu, emphasizing his absolute supremacy over all beings—whether divine, demonic, or mortal. His invincibility ensures that no force can disrupt his cosmic authority, reaffirming his role as the guardian of balance and righteousness in the universe.

206. Śasta: One who instructs and directs all through the scriptures.

207. Vishrutatma: One who is specially known through signifying terms like Truth, Knowledge, etc.

208. Surārihā: One who destroys the enemies of Suras or Devas.

gururgurutamō dhāmaḥ satyaḥ satyaparākramaḥ, nimiṣō nimiṣaḥ sragvī vācaspatirudāradhīḥ. (23)

209. Guruḥ: The greatest teacher.

210. Gurutamaḥ: One who is the teacher of all forms of knowledge.

211. Dhāma: The Supreme Light.

212. Satyaḥ: One who is embodied as virtue of truth specially.

213. Satyaparākamaḥ: One of unfailing valour.

214. Nimiṣaḥ: One whose eye-lids are closed in Yoga-nidra.

215. Animiṣaḥ: One who is ever awake.

216. Sragvī: One who has on Him the necklace called Vaijayanti, which is strung with the subtle aspects of the five elements.

217. Vācaspatir-udāradhīḥ: Lord Vishnu is revered as Vācaspatir-udāradhīḥ, signifying his mastery over speech and wisdom. He is called Vācaspati because he governs Vak, the divine essence of words, knowledge, and expression. His intellect, vast and all-encompassing, perceives everything without limitation, earning him the title Udaradhīḥ. These attributes together form a single divine name, underscoring his omniscient nature and supreme wisdom.

agraṇīrgrāmaṇīḥ śrīmān nyāyō netā samīraṇaḥ,

sahasramūrdhā viśvātmā sahasrākṣaḥ sahasrapāt. (24)

218. Agraṇīḥ: One who leads all liberation-seekers to the highest status.

219. Grāmaṇīḥ: One who has the command over Bhutagrama or the collectivity of all beings.

220. Śrīmān: One more resplendent than everything.

221. Nyāyaḥ: The consistency which runs through all ways of knowing and which leads one to the truth of non-duality.

222. Netā: One who moves this world of becoming.

223. Sahasramūrdhā: One with a thousand, i.e. innumerable,heads.

224. Samīraṇaḥ: One who in the form of breath keeps all living beings functioning.

225. Viśvātmā: The soul of the universe.

226. Sahasrākṣaḥ: One with a thousand or innumerable eyes.

227. Sahasrapāt: One with a thousand, i.e. innumerable legs.

āvartanō nivṛttātmā saṁvṛtaḥ saṁpramardanaḥ, ahaḥ saṁvartakō vahniranilō dharaṇīdharaḥ. (25)

228. Āvrtanaḥ: One who whirls round and round the Samsara-chakra, the wheel of Samsara or worldy existence.

229. Nivṛttātmā: One whose being is free or untouched by the bondage of Samsara.

230. Saṁvṛtaḥ: One who is covered by all-covering Avidya or ignorance.

231. Sampramardanaḥ: One who delivers destructive blows on all beings through His Vibhutis (power manifestation like Rudra, Yama etc.).

232. Ahaḥ-saṁvartakaḥ: The Lord who, as the sun, regulates the succession of day and night.

233. Vahniḥ: One who as fire carries the offerings made to the Devas in sacrifices.

234. Anilaḥ: One who has no fixed residence.

235. Dharaṇī-dharaḥ: One who supports the worlds, Adisesha, elephants of the quarters, etc.

suprasādaḥ prasannātmā viśvadhṛgviśvabhugvibhuḥ, satkartā satkṛtaḥ

sādhurjahnurnārāyaṇō naraḥ. (26)

236. Suprasādaḥ: One whose Prasada or mercy is uniquely wonderful, because He gives salvation to Sisupala and others who try to harm Him.

237. Prasannātmā: One whose mind is never contaminated by Rajas or Tamas.

238. Viśvadhṛg: One who holds the universe by his power.

239. Viśvabhug: One who eats up or enjoys or protects the worlds.

240. Vibhuḥ: One who takes various forms

241. Satkartā: One who offers benefits.

242. Satkṛtaḥ: One who is adored even by those who deserve adoration.

243. Sādhuḥ: One who acts according to justice.

244. Jahnuḥ: One who dissolves all beings in oneself at the time of dissolution.

245. Nārāyaṇaḥ: Nara means Atman. Narayana, that is, one having His residence in all beings.

246. Naraḥ: He directs everything, the eternal Paramatma is called Nara.

asaṅkhyeyō'prameyātmā viśiṣṭaḥ śiṣṭakṛcchuciḥ, siddhārthaḥ

siddhasaṅkalpaḥ siddhidaḥ

siddhisādhanaḥ. (27)

247. Asaṅkhyeyaḥ: One who has no Sankhya or differences of name and form.

248. Aprameyātmā: One whose nature cannot be grasped by any of the means of knowledge.

249. Viśiṣṭaḥ: One who excels everything.

250. Śiṣṭakṛt: One who commands everything. Or one who protects shishtas or good men.

251. Suciḥ: The Sanskrit word Suciḥ translates to "pure" or "spotless," emphasizing Vishnu's absolute purity in form,

thought, and action. It reflects his unblemished nature, free from any worldly impurities, and highlights his role as the ultimate source of divine sanctity. This name reinforces Vishnu's transcendence beyond material limitations, making him the embodiment of spiritual perfection.

252. Siddhārthaḥ: One whose object is always fulfilled.

253. Siddhasaṅkalpaḥ: One whose resolutions are always fulfilled.

254. Siddhidaḥ: One who bestows Siddhi or fulfillment on all who practise disciplines, in accordance with their eligibility.

255. Siddhisādhanaḥ: One who brings fulfillment to works that deserve the same.

vṛṣāhī vṛṣabhō viṣṇurvṛṣaparvā vṛṣōdaraḥ, vardhanō vardhamānaśca

viviktaḥ śrutisāgaraḥ. (28)

256. Vṛṣāhī: Vrusha means dharma or merit.

257. Vṛṣābhaḥ: One who showers on the devotees all that they pray for.

258. Viṣṇuḥ: One who pervades everything.

259. Vṛṣaparva: One who has given as steps (Parvas), observances of the nature of Dharma, to those who want to attain the supreme state.

260. Vṛṣodaraḥ: One whose abdomen showers offspring.

261. Vardhanaḥ: One who increases the ecstasy of His devotees

262. Vardhamānaḥ: One who multiplies in the form of the universe.

263. Viviktaḥ: One who is untouched and unaffected.

264. Śrutisāgaraḥ: One to whom all the shruti or Vedic words and sentences flow.

subhujō durdharō vāgmī mahendrō vasudō vasuḥ, naikarūpō bṛhadrūpaḥ

śipiviṣṭaḥ prakāśanaḥ. (29)

265. Subhujaḥ: One possessing excellent arms that protect the worlds.

266. Durdharaḥ: One who holds up the universe – a work which none else can do.

267. Vāgmi: One from whom the words constituting the Veda come out.

268. Mahendraḥ: The great Lord, that is, the Supreme Being, who is the God of all gods.

269. Vasudaḥ: One who bestows riches.

270. Vasuḥ: One who is himself the Vasu.

271. Naikarūpaḥ: One who is without an exclusive form.

272. Bṛhadrūpaḥ: One who has adopted mysterious forms like that of a Boar.

273. Śipiviṣṭaḥ: Shipi means cow. One who resides in cows as Yajna.

274. Prakāśanaḥ: One who illumines everything.

ōjastejōdyutidharaḥ prakāśātmā pratāpanaḥ,

ṛddhaḥ spaṣṭākṣarō mantraścandrāṁśurbhāskaradyutiḥ. (30)

275. Ōjas-tejō-dyuti-dharaḥ: One who is endowed with strength, vigour and brilliance.
276. Prakāśātmā: One whose form is radiant.
277. Pratāpanaḥ: One who warms the world through the power manifestations like the Sun.
278. Ṛddhaḥ: This name signifies prosperity, growth, and divine abundance. The Sanskrit term Ṛddhaḥ translates to "one who is ever-flourishing and exalted," highlighting Vishnu's limitless expansion and supreme richness in both material and spiritual realms. As the eternal source of prosperity, Vishnu embodies unwavering abundance, ensuring the well-being of all creation. This name reinforces his unmatched greatness, portraying him as the ultimate sustainer who nurtures the universe with infinite wisdom, wealth, and divine grace.
279. Spaṣṭākṣaraḥ: He is so called because Omkara, the manifesting sound of the Lord, is Spashta or high pitched.
280. Mantraḥ: One who manifests as the Mantras of the Rk, Sama, Yajus etc., or one who is known through Mantras.
281. Candrāṁśuḥ: He is called 'Chandramshu' or moonlight because just as the moon-light gives relief to men burnt in the heat of the sun, He gives relief and shelter to those who are subjected to the heat of Samsara.

282. Bhāskara-dyutiḥ: He who has the effulgence of the sun.

amṛtāṁśūdbhavō bhānuḥ śaśabinduḥ sureśvaraḥ, auṣadhaṁ jagataḥ setuḥ satyadharmaparākramaḥ. (31)

283. Amṛtāṁśūdbhavaḥ: The Paramatman from whom Amrutamshu or the Moon originated at the time of the churning of the Milk-ocean.

284. Bhānuḥ: One who shines.

285. Śaśabinduḥ: The word means one who has the mark of the hare, that is the Moon.

286. Sureśvaraḥ: One who is the Lord of all Devas and those who do good.

287. Auṣadham: One who is the Aushadha or medicine for the great disease of Samsara.

288. Jagataḥ setuḥ: One who is the aid to go across the ocean of Samsara.

289. Satya-dharma-parākramaḥ: One whose excellences like righteousness, omniscience, puissance, etc. are all true.

bhūtabhavyabhavannāthaḥ pavanaḥ pāvano'nalaḥ, kāmahā kāmakṛtkāntaḥ kāmaḥ kāmapradaḥ prabhuḥ. (32)

290. Bhūta-bhavya-bhavan-nāthaḥ: One who is the master for all the beings of the past, future and present.
291. Pavanaḥ: One who is the purifier.
292. Pāvanaḥ: One who causes movement.
293. Analaḥ: The Jivatma is called Anala because it recognizes Ana or Prana as Himself.
294. Kāmahā: One who destroys the desire-nature in seekers after liberation.
295. Kāmakṛt: One who fulfils the wants of pure minded devotees.
296. Kantaḥ: One who is extremely beautiful.
297. Kāmaḥ: One who is sought after by those who desire to attain the four supreme values of life.
298. Kāmapradaḥ: One who liberally fulfils the desires of devotees.
299. Prabhuḥ: One who surpasses all.

yugādikṛdyugāvartō naikamāyō mahāśanaḥ,

adṛśyō vyaktarūpaśca sahasrajidanantajit. (33)

300. Yugādikṛd: One who is the cause of periods of time like Yuga.

301. Yugāvartaḥ: One who as time causes the repetition of the four Yugas beginning with Satya Yuga.

302. Naikamāyaḥ: One who can assume numerous forms of Maya, not one only.

303. Mahāśanaḥ: One who consumes everything at the end of a Kalpa.

304. Adṛśyaḥ: One who cannot be grasped by any of the five organs of knowledge.

305. Vyaktarūpaḥ: He is so called because his gross form as universe can be clearly perceived.

306. Sahasrajit: One who is victorious over innumerable enemies of the Devas in battle.

307. Anantajit: One who, being endowed with all powers, is victorious at all times over everything.

iṣṭō'viśiṣṭaḥ śiṣṭeṣṭaḥ śikhaṇḍī nahuṣō vṛṣaḥ,

krōdhahā krōdhakṛtkartā viśvabāhurmahīdharaḥ. (34)

308. Iṣṭaḥ: One who is dear to all because He is of the nature of supreme Bliss.

309. Aviśiṣṭaḥ: One who resides within all.

310. Śiṣṭeṣṭaḥ: One who is dear to shishta or Knowing Ones.

311. Śikhaṇḍī: Sikhanda means feather of a peacock. One who used it as a decoration for His crown when he adopted the form of a cowherd (Gopa).

312. Nahuṣaḥ: One who binds all beings by Maya the root 'nah' means bondage.

313. Vṛṣaḥ: One who is of the form of Dharma.

314. Krōdhahā: One who eradicates anger in virtuous people.

315. Krōdhakṛt-kartā: One who generates Krodha or anger in evil people.

316. Viśvabāhuḥ: One who is the support of all or one who has got all beings as His arms.

317. Mahīdharaḥ: Mahi means both earth and worship. So the name means one who supports the earth or receives all forms of worship.

acyutaḥ prathitaḥ prāṇaḥ prāṇadō vāsavānujaḥ,

apāṁnidhiradhiṣṭhānamapramattaḥ pratiṣṭhitaḥ. (35)

318. Acyutaḥ: One who is without the six transformations beginning with birth.

319. Prathitaḥ: One who is famous because of His works like creation of the worlds etc.

320. Prāṇaḥ: One who as Hiranyagarbha endows all beings with Prana.

321. Prāṇadaḥ: One who bestows Prana, that is, strength, on Devas and Asuras and also destroys them by withdrawing it.

322. Vāsavānujaḥ: One who was born as younger brother of Indra (Vasava) in His incarnation as Vamana.

323. Apāṁ nidhiḥ: The word means collectivity of water or the ocean.

324. Adhiṣṭhānam: The seat or support for everything.

325. Apramattaḥ: One who is always vigilant in awarding the fruits of actions to those who are entiled to them.

326. Pratiṣṭhitaḥ: One who is supported and established in His own greatness.

skandaḥ skandadharō dhuryō varadō vāyuvāhanaḥ, vāsudevō

bṛhadbhānurādidevaḥ purandaraḥ. (36)

327. Skandaḥ: One who drives everything as air.

328. Skanda-dharaḥ: One who supports Skanda or the righteous path.

329. Dhuryaḥ: One who bears the weight of the burden of all beings in the form of birth etc.

330. Varadaḥ: One who gives boons.

331. Vāyuvāhanaḥ: One who vibrates the seven Vayus or atmospheres beginning with Avaha.

332. Vāsudevaḥ: One who is both Vasu and Deva.

333. Bṛhadbhānuḥ: The great brilliance.

334. Ādidevaḥ: The Divinity who is the source of all Devas.

335. Purandaraḥ: One who destroys the cities of the enemies of Devas.

aśōkastāraṇastāraḥ śūraḥ śaurirjaneśvaraḥ,

anukūlaḥ śatāvartaḥ padmī padmanibhekṣaṇaḥ. (37)

336. Aśokaḥ: One without the six defects – sorrow, infatuation, hunger, thirst, birth and death.

337. Tāraṇaḥ: One who uplifts beings from the ocean of samsara.

338. Tāraḥ: One who liberates beings from the fear of residence in the womb, birth, old age, death etc.

339. Śūraḥ: One of great prowess, that is, who fulfils the four supreme satisfactions of life – Dharma, Artha, Kama and Moksha.

340. Śauriḥ: One who as Krishna as the son of Sura, that is Vasudeva.

341. Janeśvaraḥ: The Lord of all beings.

342. Anukūlaḥ: One who, being the Atman of all beings, is

favorable to all, for no one will act against oneself.

343. Śatāvartaḥ: One who has had several Avataras or incarnations.

344. Padmī: One having Padma or lotus in his hands.

345. Padma-nibhekṣaṇaḥ: One with eyes resembling lotus.

padmanābhōravindākṣaḥ padmagarbhaḥ śarīrabhṛt, maharddhir ṛddhō

vṛddhātmā mahākṣō garuḍadhvajaḥ. (38)

346. Padma-nābhaḥ: One who resides in the Nabhi or the central part of the heart-lotus.

347. Aravindākṣaḥ: One whose eyes resemble Aravinda or the Lotus.

348. Padma-garbhaḥ: One who is fit to be worshipped in the middle of the heart-lotus.

349. Śarīra-bhṛt: One who supports the bodies of beings, strengthening them in the form of Anna (Food) and Prana.

350. Mahardhi: One who has enormous Ruddhi or prosperity.

351. Ṛddhaḥ: One who is seen as standing in the form of the world.

352. Vṛddhātmā: One whose Atma or body is Vruddha or ancient.

353. Mahākṣaḥ: One who has got two or many glorious eyes.

354. Garuḍa-dhvajaḥ: One who has got Garuda as his flag.

atulaḥ śarabhō bhīmaḥ samayajñō havirhariḥ, sarvalakṣaṇalakṣaṇyō lakṣmīvān samitiñjayaḥ. (39)

355. Atulaḥ: One who cannot be compared to anything else.

356. Śarabhaḥ: The body is called 'Sara' as it is perishable.

357. Bhīmaḥ: One of whom everyone is afraid.

358. Samayajñaḥ: One who knows the time for creation, sustentation and dissolution.

359. Havir-hariḥ: One who takes the portion of offerings (Havis) in Yajnas.

360. Sarva-lakṣaṇa-lakṣaṇyaḥ: The supreme knowledge obtained through all criteria of knowledge i.e. Paramatma.

361. Lakṣmīvān: One on whose chest the Goddess Lakshmi is always residing.

362. Samitiñjayaḥ: One who is vicotious in Samiti or war.

vikṣarō rōhitō mārgō heturdamodarassahaḥ,

mahīdharō mahābhāgō vegavānamitāśanaḥ. (40)

363. Vikṣaraḥ: The Sanskrit term Vikṣaraḥ translates to "One who is beyond decay or destruction," highlighting Vishnu's unchanging and indestructible nature. Unlike the material world, which undergoes constant transformation and dissolution, Vishnu remains eternal, unaffected by time or cosmic cycles. This name reinforces his supreme permanence, portraying him as the absolute, ever-existing force that sustains the universe.

364. Rōhitaḥ: One who assumed the form of a kind of fish called Rohita.

365. Mārgaḥ: One who is sought after by persons seeking Moksha or Liberation.

366. Hetuḥ: One who is both the instrumental and the material cause of the universe.

367. Damodaraḥ: One who has very benevolent mind because of disciplines like self-control.

368. Sahaḥ: One who subordinates everything.

369. Mahīdharaḥ: One who props up the earth in the form of mountain.

370. Mahābhāgaḥ: He who, taking a body by His own will, enjoys supreme felicities.

371. Vegavān: One of tremendous speed.

372. Amitāśanaḥ: He who consumes all the worlds at the time of Dissolution.

udbhavaḥ, kṣōbhaṇō devaḥ śrīgarbhaḥ parameśvaraḥ, karaṇaṁ kāraṇaṁ kartā vikartā gahanō guhaḥ. (41)

373. Udbhavaḥ: One who is the material cause of creation.

374. Kṣōbhaṇaḥ: One who at the time of creation entered into the Purusha and Prakriti and caused agitation.

375. Devaḥ: 'Divyati' means sports oneself through creation and other cosmic activities.

376. Śrīgarbhaḥ: One in whose abdomen (Garbha) Shri or His unique manifestation as Samsara has its existence.

377. Parameśvaraḥ: 'Parama' means the supreme. 'Ishvarah' means one who hold sway over all beings.

378. Karaṇam: He who is the most important factor in the generation of this universe.

379. Kāraṇam: The Cause – He who causes others to act.

380. Kartā: One who is free and is therefore one's own master.

381. Vikartā: One who makes this unique universe.

382. Gahanaḥ: One whose nature, greatness and actions cannot be known by anybody.

383. Guhaḥ: One who hides one's own nature with the help of His power of Maya.

vyavasāyō vyavasthānaḥ saṁsthānaḥ sthānadō dhruvaḥ, pararddhiḥ

paramaspaṣṭastuṣṭaḥ puṣṭaḥ śubhekṣaṇaḥ. (42)

384. Vyavasāyaḥ: One who is wholly of the nature of knowledge.

385. Vyavasthānaḥ: He in whom the orderly regulation of the universe rests.

386. Sāṁsthānaḥ: One in whom all beings dwell in the states of dissolution.

387. Sthānadaḥ: One who gives their particular status to persons like Dhruva according to their Karma.

388. Dhruvaḥ: One who is indestructible.

389. Pararddhiḥ: One who possesses lordliness of this most exalted type.

390. Paramaspaṣṭaḥ: One in whom 'Para' or supremely glorious 'Ma' or Lakshmi dwells. Or one who is the greatest of all beings without any other's help.

391. Tuṣṭaḥ: One who is of the nature of supreme.

392. Puṣṭaḥ: One who in fills everything.

393. Śubhekṣaṇaḥ: One whose Ikshanam or vision bestows good on all beings that is, gives liberation to those who want Moksha and enjoyments to those who are after it, and also cuts asunder the knots of the heart by eliminating all doubts.

rāmō virāmō virajō mārgō neyō nayōnayaḥ,

vīraḥ śaktimatāṁ śreṣṭhō dharmō dharmaviduttamaḥ. (43)

394. Ramaḥ: The eternally blissful on in whom the Yogis find delight.

395. Virāmaḥ: One in whom the Virama or end of all beings takes place.

396. Virajaḥ: One in whom the desire for enjoyments has ceased

397. Mārgaḥ: The path.

398. Neyaḥ: One who directs or leads the Jiva to the Supreme Being through spiritual realization.

399. Nayaḥ: One who leads, that is, who is the leader in the form of spiritual illumination.

400. Anayaḥ: One for whom there is no leader.

401. Vīraḥ: One who is valorous.

402. Śaktimatāṁ śreṣṭhaḥ: One who is the most powerful among all powerful beings like Brahma.

403. Dharmaḥ: One who supports all beings.

404. Dharma-viduttamaḥ: The greatest of knower of Dharma. He is called so because all the scriptures consisting of Shrutis and Smrutis form His commandments.

vaikuṇṭhaḥ puruṣaḥ prāṇaḥ prāṇadaḥ praṇavaḥ pṛthuḥ, hiraṇyagarbhaḥ

śatrughnō vyāptō vāyuradhōkṣajaḥ. (44)

405. Vaikuṇṭhaḥ: The bringing together of the diversified categories is Vikuntha. He who is the agent of it is Vaikunthah.

406. Puruṣaḥ: One who existed before everything.

407. Prāṇaḥ: One who lives as Kshetrajana (knower in the body) or one who functions in the form of vital force called Prana.

408. Prāṇadaḥ: One who is the giver of life.

409. Praṇavaḥ: One who is praised or to whom prostration is made with Om.

410. Pṛthuḥ: One who has expanded himself as the world.

411. Hiraṇyagarbhaḥ: He who was the cause of the golden-coloured egg out of which Brahma was born.

412. Śatrughnaḥ: One who destroys the enemies of the Devas.

413. Vyāptaḥ: One who as the cause pervades all effects.

414. Vāyuḥ: One who moves towards His devotees.

415. Adhokṣajaḥ: He is Adhokshaja because he undergoes no degeneration from His original nature.

ṛtuḥ sudarśanaḥ kālaḥ parameṣṭhī parigrahaḥ, ugraḥ saṁvatsarō dakṣō

viśrāmō viśvadakṣiṇaḥ. (45)

416. Ṛtuḥ: One who is of the nature of Kala (time) which is indicated by the word Ritu or season.

417. Sudarśanaḥ: One whose Darshana or vision that is knowledge, bestows the most auspicious fruit Moksha.

418. Kālaḥ: One who measures and sets a limit to everything.

419. Parameṣṭhī: One who dwells in his supreme greatness in the sky of the heart.

420. Parigrahaḥ: One who, being everywhere, is grasped on all sides by those who seek refuge in Him. Or one who grasps or receives the offerings made by devotees.

421. Ugraḥ: One who is the cause of fear even to beings like Sun.

422. Saṁvatsaraḥ: One in whom all beings reside.

423. Dakṣaḥ: One who augments in the form of the world.

424. Viśrāmaḥ: One who bestows Vishrama or liberation to aspirants who seek relief from the ocean of Samsara with its waves of various tribulations in the form of Hunger, Thirst etc., and difficulties like Avidya, pride, infatuation etc.

425. Viśvadakṣiṇaḥ: One who is more skilled (Daksha) than everyone. Or One who is proficient in everything.

vistāraḥ sthāvaraḥsthāṇuḥ pramāṇaṁ bījamavyayam, arthōnarthō

mahākōśō mahābhōgō mahādhanaḥ. (46)

426. Vistāraḥ: One in whom all the worlds have attained manifestation.

427. Sthāvaraḥ-sthāṇuḥ: One who is firmly established is Sthavara, and in whom long lasting entities like earth are established in Sthanu. The Lord is both these.

428. Pramāṇaṁ: One who is of the nature of pure consciousness.

429. Bījamavyayam: One who is the seed or cause of Samsara without Himself undergoing any change.

430. Arthaḥ: One who is sought (Arthita) by all, as He is of the nature of bliss.

431. Anarthaḥ: One who, being self-fulfilled, has no other Artha or end to seek.

432. Mahākōśaḥ: One who has got as His covering the great Koshas like Annamaya, Pranamaya etc.

433. Mahābhōgaḥ: One who has Bliss as the great source of enjoyment.

434. Mahādhanaḥ: One who has got the whole universe as the wealth (Dhana) for His enjoyment.

anirviṇṇaḥ sthaviṣṭhōbhūrdharmayūpō mahāmakhaḥ.

nakṣatranemirnakṣatrī kṣamaḥ kṣāmaḥ samīhanaḥ. (47)

435. Anirviṇṇaḥ: One who is never heedless, because He is ever self-fulfilled.

436. Sthaviṣṭhaḥ: One of huge proportions, because He is in the form of cosmic person.

437. Abhūḥ: One without birth. Or one has no existence.

438. Dharma-yūpaḥ: The sacrificial post for Dharmas, that is, one to whom all the forms of Dharma, which are His own form of worship, are attached, just as a sacrificial animal is attached to a Yupa or a sacrificial post.

439. Mahāmakhaḥ: One by offering sacrifices to whom, those sacrifices deserve to be called great, because they well give the fruit of Nirvana.

440. Nakṣatra-nemiḥ: The heart of all nakshatras.

441. Nakṣatrī: He is in the form of the nakshatra, Moon.

442. Kṣamaḥ: One who is clever in everything.

443. Kṣāmaḥ: One who remains in the state of pure self after all

the modifications of the mind have dwindled.

444. Samīhanaḥ: One who exerts well for creation, etc.

yajña ijyō mahejyaśca kratuḥ satraṁ satāṁ gatiḥ,

sarvadarśī vimuktātmā sarvajñō jñānamuttamam. (48)

445. Yajñaḥ: One who is all-knowing.

446. Ijayaḥ: One who is fit to be worshipped in sacrifices.

447. Mahejyaḥ: He who, of all deities worshipped, is alone capable of giving the blessing of liberation.

448. Kratuḥ: A Yajna in which there is a sacrificial post is Kratu.

449. Satraṁ: One who is of the nature of ordained Dharma.

450. Satāṁ-gatiḥ: One who is the sole support for holy men who are seekers of Moksha.

451. Sarva-darśī: One who by His inborn insight is able to see all good and evil actions of living beings.

452. Vimuktātmā: One who is naturally free.

453. Sarvagñaḥ: One who is all and also the knower of all.

454. Jñānam-uttamam: That consciousness which is superior to all, birthless, unlimited by time and space and the cause of all achievements.

suvrataḥ sumukhaḥ sūkṣmaḥ sughōṣaḥ sukhadaḥ suhṛt,

manōharō jitakrōdhō vīrabāhurvidāraṇaḥ. (49)

455. Suvrataḥ: One who has taken the magnanimous vow to save all refuge-seekers.

456. Sumukhaḥ: One with a pleasant face.

457. Sūkṣmaḥ: One who is subtle because He is without any gross causes like sound etc.

458. Sughōṣaḥ: One whose auspicious sound is the Veda. Or one who has got a deep and sonorous sound like the clouds.

459. Sukhadaḥ: One who gives happiness to good people.

460. Suhṛt: One who helps without looking for any return.

461. Manōharaḥ: One who attracts the mind by His incomparable blissful nature.

462. Jitakrōdhaḥ: One who has overcome anger.

463. Vīrabāhuḥ: One whose arms are capable of heroic deeds as demonstrated in his destruction of Asuras for establishing Vedic Dharma.

464. Vidāraṇaḥ: One who destroys those who live contrary to Dharma.

svāpanaḥ svavaśo vyāpī naikātmā naikakarmakṛt,

vatsaro vatsalo vatsī ratnagarbho dhaneśvaraḥ. (50)

465. Svāpanaḥ: One who enfolds the Jivas in the sleep of Ajnana.

466. Svavaśaḥ: One who is dominated by oneself and not anything else, as He is the cause of the whole cosmic process.

467. Vyāpī: One who interpenetrates everything like Akasha.

468. Naikātmā: One who manifests in different forms as the subsidiary agencies causing the various cosmic processes.

469. Naikakarmakṛt: One who engages in innumerable activities in the process of creation, sustentation, etc.

470. Vatsaraḥ: One in whom everything dwells.

471. Vatsalaḥ: One who has love for His devotees.

472. Vatsī: One who protects those who are dear to Him.

473. Ratnagarbhaḥ: The Ocean is so called because gems are found in its depths. As the Lord has taken the form of the ocean, He is called by this name.

474. Dhaneśvaraḥ: One who is the Lord of all wealth.

dharmagubdharmakṛddharmī sadasatkṣaramakṣaram, avijñātā

sahasrāṁśurvidhātā kṛtalakṣaṇaḥ. (51)

475. Dharmagub: One who protects Dharma.

476. Dharmakṛd: Though above. Dharma and Adharma, He performs Dharma in order to keep up the traditions in respect of it.

477. Dharmī: One who upholds Dharma.

478. Sat: The Parabrahman who is of the nature of truth.

479. Asat: As the Aparabrahma has manifested as the world He is called Asat (not having reality).

480. Kṣaram: All beings subjected to change.

481. Akṣaram: The changeless one.

482. Aviñātā: One who is without the attributes of a Jiva or vigyata like sense of agency, etc.

483. Sahasrāṁśuḥ: One with numerous rays, that is the Sun.

484. Vidhātā: One who is the unique support of all agencies like Ananta who bear the whole universe.

485. Kṛtalakṣaṇaḥ: One who is of the nature of conscousness.

gabhastinemiḥ sattvasthaḥ siṁhō bhūtamaheśvaraḥ, ādidevō mahādevō

deveśō devabhṛdguruḥ. (52)

486. Gabhastinemiḥ: He who dwells in the middle of Gabhasti or rays as the Sun.

487. Sattvasthaḥ: One who dwells specially in sattvaguna, which is luminous by nature.

488. Simhaḥ: One who ahs irresistible power like a lion.

489. Bhūtamaheśvaraḥ: The supreme Lord of all beings.

490. Ādidevaḥ: He who is the first of all beings.

491. Mahādevaḥ: One whose greatness consists in His supreme self-knowledge.

492. Deveśaḥ: One who is the lord of all Devas, being the most important among them.

493. Devabhṛd-guruḥ: Indra who governs the Devas is Devabhrut. The Lord is even that Indra's controller (Guru).

uttarō gōpatirgōptā jñānagamyaḥ purātanaḥ,

śarīrabhūtabhṛdbhōktā kapīndrō bhūridakṣiṇaḥ. (53)

494. Uttaraḥ: One who is Uttirna or liberated from Samsara.

495. Gōpatiḥ: Krishna who tends the cattle in the form of a Gopa. One who is the master of the earth.

496. Gōptā: One who is the protector of all beings.

497. Jñānagamyaḥ: The Lord cannot be known through Karma or a combination of Karma and Jyana.

498. Purātanaḥ: One who is not limited by time and who existed before anything else.

499. Śarīrabhūtabhṛd: One who is the master of the five Bhutas (elements) of which the body is made.

500. Bhōktā: One who protects. Or one who is the enjoyer of infinite bliss.

501. Kapīndraḥ: Kapi means Varah (boar). The word means, the Lord who is Indra and also one who manifested as Varaha or the Boar in one of the incarnations. Or it signifies His Rama incarnation in which He played the role of the master of the monkeys.

502. Bhūridakṣiṇaḥ: One to whom numerous Dakshinas or votive offerings are made in Yajnas.

somapo'mṛtapaḥ sōmaḥ purujit purusattamaḥ,

vinayō jayaḥ satyasandhō dāśārhassātvatāṁ patiḥ. (54)

503. Sōmapaḥ: One who drinks the Soma in all Yajnas in the form of the Devata.

504. Amṛtapaḥ: One who drinks the drink of immortal Bliss which is of one's own nature.

505. Sōmaḥ: One who as the moon invigorates the plants.

506. Purujit: One who gains victory over numerous people.

507. Purushottamaḥ: As His form is of cosmic dimension, He is Puru or great, and as He is the most important of all, He is Sattama.

508. Vinayaḥ: One who inflicts Vinaya or punishment on evil ones.

509. Jayaḥ: One who is victorious over all beings.

510. Satyasandhaḥ: One whose 'Sandha' or resolve becomes always true.

511. Dāśārhaḥ: Dasha means charitable offering. Therefore, He to whom charitable offerings deserve to be made.

512. Sātvatāṁ-patiḥ: 'Satvatam' is the name of a Tantra. So the one who gave it out or commented upon it.

jīvo vinayitā sākṣī mukundo'mitavikramaḥ,

ambhonidhiranantātmā mahodadhiśayo'ntakaḥ. (55)

513. Jīvaḥ: One who as the Kshetragya or knower of the field or the body, is associated with the Pranas.

514. Vinayitā-sākṣī: One who witnesses the Vinayita or worshipful attitude of all devotees.

515. Mukundaḥ: One who bestows Mukti or Liberation.

516. Amitavikramaḥ: One whose three strides were limitless.

517. Ambhōnidhiḥ: One in whom the Ambas or all beings from Devas down dwell.

518. Anantātmā: One who cannot be determined by space, time and causation.

519. Mahōdadhi-śayaḥ: One who lies in the water of Cosmic Dissolution into which all entities in the universe have been dissolved.

520. Antakaḥ: One who brings about the end of all beings.

ajō mahārhaḥ svābhāvyō jitāmitraḥ pramōdanaḥ,

ānandō nandanō nandaḥ satyadharmā trivikramaḥ. (56)

521. Ajaḥ: 'A' means Mahavishnu. So the word means one who is born of Vishnu i.e. Kama Deva.

522. Mahārhaḥ: One who is fit for worship.

523. Svābhāvyaḥ: Being eternally perfect He is naturally without a beginning.

524. Jitāmitraḥ: One who has conquered the inner enemies like attachment, anger, etc. as also external enemies like Ravana, Kumbhakarna etc.

525. Pramōdanaḥ: One who is always joyous as He is absorbed in immortal Bliss.

526. Ānandaḥ: One whose form is Ananda or Bliss.

527. Nandanaḥ: One who gives delight.

528. Nandaḥ: One endowed with all perfections.

529. Satyadharmā: One whose knowledge and other attributes are true.

530. Trivikramaḥ: One whose three strides covered the whole world.

maharṣiḥ kapilācāryaḥ kṛtajñō medinīpatiḥ,

tripadastridaśādhyakṣō mahāśṛṅgaḥ kṛtāntakṛt. (57)

531. Maharṣiḥ Kapilācāryaḥ: Kapila is called Maharshi because he was master of all the Vedas.
532. Kṛtajñaḥ: Kruta means the world because it is of the nature of an effect.
533. Medinīpatiḥ: One who is the Lord of the earth.
534. Tripadaḥ: One having three strides.
535. Tridaśādhyakṣaḥ: One who is the witness of the three states of waking, dream and sleep, which spring from the influence of the Gunas.
536. Mahāśṛṅgaḥ: One with a great antenna.
537. Kṛtānta-kṛt: One who brings about the destruction of the Kruta or the manifested condition of the universe.

mahāvarāhō gōvindaḥ suṣeṇaḥ kanakāṅgadī,

guhyō gabhīrō gahanō guptaścakragadādharaḥ. (58)

538. Mahā-varāhaḥ: The great Cosmic Boar.

539. Gōvindaḥ: 'Go' means Words, that is the Vedic sentences. He who is known by them is Gōvindaḥ.

540. Suṣeṇaḥ: One who has got about Him an armed guard in the shape of His eternal associates.

541. Kanakāṅgadī: One who has Angadas (armlets) made of gold.

542. Guhyaḥ: One who is to be known by the Guhya or the esoteric knowledge conveyed by the Upanishads. Or one who is hidden in the Guha or heart.

543. Gabhīraḥ: One who is of profound majesty because of attributes like omniscience, lordliness, strength, prowess, etc.

544. Gahanaḥ: One who could be entered into only with great difficulty. One who is the witness of the three states of waking, dreams and sleep as also their absence.

545. Guptaḥ: One who is not an object of words, thought, etc.

546. Chakra-gadā-dharaḥ: One who has discus and Gada in hand.

vedhāḥ svāṅgo'jitaḥ kṛṣṇo dṛḍhaḥ saṅkarṣaṇo'cyutaḥ,

varuṇo vāruṇo vṛukṣaḥ puṣkarākṣo mahāmanāḥ. (59)

547. Vedhāḥ: One who does Vidhana or regulation.

548. Svāṅgaḥ: One who is oneself the participant in accomplishing works.

549. Ajitaḥ: One who has not been conquered by anyone in His various incarnations.

550. Kṛṣṇaḥ: One who is known as Krishna-dvaipayana.

551. Dṛḍhaḥ: One whose nature and capacity know no decay.

552. Saṅkarṣaṇo-acyutaḥ: Sankarshana is one who attracts to oneself all beings at the time of cosmic Dissolution and Acyuta is one who knows no fall from His real nature. They form one word with the first as the qualification – Acyuta who is Sankarshana.

553. Varuṇaḥ: The evening sun is called Varuna, because he withdraws his rays into himself.

554. Vāruṇaḥ: Vasishta or Agastya, the sons of Varuna.

555. Vṛukṣaḥ: One who is unshakable like a tree.

556. Puṣkarākṣaḥ: One who shines as the light of consciousness when meditated upon in the lotus of the heart. Or one who has eyes resembling the lotus.

557. Mahāmanāḥ: One who fulfils the three functions of creation, sustentation and dissolution of the universe by the mind alone.

bhagavān bhagahānandī vanamālī halāyudhaḥ, ādityō

jyōtirādityaḥ sahiṣṇurgatisattamaḥ. (60)

558. Bhagavān: The origin, dissolution, the bondage and salvation of creatures, knowledge, ignorance – one who knows all these is Bhagavan.

559. Bhagahā: One who withdraws the Bhagas, beginning with lordliness, into Himself at the time of dissolution.

560. Ānandī: One whose nature is Ananda (bliss).

561. Vanamālī: One who wears the floral wreath (Vanamala) called Vaijayanti, which consists of the categories of five elements.

562. Halāyudhaḥ: One who in His incarnation as Balabhadra had Hala or ploughshare as His weapon.

563. Ādityaḥ: One who was born of Aditi in His incarnation as Vamana.

564. Jyōtir-ādityaḥ: One who dwells in the brilliance of the sun's orb.

565. Sahiṣṇuḥ: One who puts up with the contraries like heat and cold.

566. Gatisattamaḥ: One who is the ultimate resort and support of all, and the greatest of all beings.

sudhanvā khaṇḍaparaśurdāruṇō draviṇapradaḥ, divaspṛk

sarvadṛgvyāsō vācaspatirayōnijaḥ. (61)

567. Sudhanvā: One who has got as His weapon the bow named Saranga of great excellence.

568. Khaṇda-paraśuḥ: The battle-axe that destroys enemies.

569. Dāruṇaḥ: One who is harsh and merciless to those who are on the evil path.

570. Draviṇapradaḥ: One who bestows the desired wealth on devotees.

571. Divah-spṛk: One who touches the heavens.

572. Sarvadṛg-vyāsaḥ: One whose comprehension includes everything in its ambit.

573. Vācaspatirayōnijaḥ: The Lord is Vachaspati because He is the master of all learning. He is Ayonija because He was not born of a mother. This forms a noun in combination with the attribute.

trisāmā sāmagaḥ sāma nirvāṇaṁ bheṣajaṁ bhiṣak,

saṁnyāsakṛcchamaśyāntō niṣṭhā śāntiḥ parāyaṇam. (62)

574. Trisāmā: One who is praised by the chanters of Sama-gana through the three Samas known as Devavratam.

575. Sāmagaḥ: One who chants the Sama-gana.

576. Sāma: Among the Vedas, I am Sama Veda.

577. Nirvāṇaṁ: That in which all miseries cease and which is of the nature of supreme bliss.

578. Bheṣajaṁ: The medicine for the disease of Samsara.

579. Bhiṣak: The Lord is called Bhishak or physician.

580. Saṁnyāsakṛt: One who instituted the fourth Ashrama of Sanyasa for the attainment of Moksha.

581. Samaḥ: One who has ordained the pacification of the mind as the most important discipline for Sannyasins (ascetics).

582. Sāntaḥ: The peaceful, being without interest in pleasures of the world.

583. Niṣṭhā: One in whom all beings remain in abeyance at the time of Pralaya.

584. Śāntiḥ: One in whom there is complete erasing of Avidya or ignorance. That is Brahman.

585. Parāyaṇam: The state, which is the highest and from which there is no return to lower states.

śubhāṅgaḥ śāntidaḥ sraṣṭā kumudaḥ kuvaleśayaḥ, gōhitō

gōpatirgōptā vṛṣabhākṣō vṛṣapriyaḥ. (63)

586. Śubhāṅgaḥ: One with a handsome form.

587. Śāntidaḥ: One who bestows shanti, that is, a state of freedom from attachment, antagonism, etc.

588. Sraṣṭā: One who brought forth everything at the start of the creative cycle.

589. Kumudaḥ: 'Ku' means the earth. One who delights in it.

590. Kuvaleśayaḥ: 'Ku' means earth. That which surrounds it is water, so 'Kuvala' means water. One who lies in water is Kuvalesaya. 'Kuvala' also means the underside of serpents. One wholies on a serpent, known as Adisesha, is Kuvalesaya.

591. Gōhitaḥ: One who protected the cows by uplifting the mount Govardhana in His incarnation as Krishna.

592. Gōpatiḥ: The Lord of the earth is Vishnu.

593. Gōptā: One who is the protector of the earth. Or one who hides Himself by His Maya.

594. Vṛṣapriyaḥ: One whose eyes can rain all desirable objects on devotees. Vrushabha means Dharma and so one whose look is Dharma.

595. Vrushapriyaḥ: One to whom Vrusha or Dharma is dear.

anivartī nivṛttātmā saṁkṣeptā kṣemakṛcchivaḥ,

śrīvatsavakṣāḥ śrīvāsaḥ śrīpatiḥ śrīmatāṁ varaḥ. (64)

596. Anivartī: One who never retreats in the battle with Asuras. Or one who, being devoted to Dharma, never abandons it.

597. Nivṛttātmā: One whose mind is naturally withdrawn from the

objects of senses.

598. Saṁkṣeptā: One who at the time of cosmic dissolution contracts the expansive universe into a subtle state.

599. Kṣemakṛt: One who gives Kshema or protection to those that go to him.

600. Śivaḥ: One who purifies everyone by the very utterance of His name.

601. Śrīvatsavakṣāḥ: One on whose chest there is a mark called Shrivasta.

602. Śrīvāsaḥ: One on whose chest Shridevi always dwells.

603. Śrīpatiḥ: One whom at the time of the churning of the Milk Ocean Shridevi chose as her consort, rejecting all other Devas and Asuras. Or Shri mean supreme Cosmic Power. The Lord is the master of that Power.

604. Śrīmatāṁ-varaḥ: One who is supreme over all deities like Brahma who are endowed with power and wealth of the Vedas.

śrīdaḥ śrīśaḥ śrīnivāsaḥ śrīnidhiḥ śrīvibhāvanaḥ, śrīdharaḥ

śrīkaraḥ śreyaḥ śrīmān lōkatrayāśrayaḥ. (65)

605. Śrīdaḥ: One who bestows prosperity on devotees.

606. Śrīśaḥ: One who is Lord of the Goddess Shri.

607. Śrīnivāsaḥ: Shri here denotes men with Shri, that is, virtue and power. He who dwells in such men is Shrinivasa.

608. Śrīnidhiḥ: One who is the seat of all Shri, that is, virtues and powers.

609. Śrīvibhāvanaḥ: One who grants every form of prosperity and virtue according to their Karma.

610. Śrīdharaḥ: One who bears on His chest Shri who is the mother of all.

611. Śrīkaraḥ: One who makes devotees – those who praise, think about Him and worship Him – into virtuous and powerful beings.

612. Śreyaḥ: 'Shreyas' means the attainment of what is un-decaying good and happiness. Such a state is the nature of the Lord.

613. Śrīmān: One in whom there are all forms of Shri that is power, virtue, beauty etc.

614. Lōkatrayāśrayaḥ: One who is the support of all the three worlds.

svakṣaḥ svaṅgaḥ śatānaṅdō naṅdirjyōtirgaṇeśvaraḥ,

vijitātmā vidheyātmā satkīrtiśchinnasaṁśayaḥ. (66)

615. Svakṣaḥ: One who's Akshas (eyes) are handsome like lotus flowers.

616. Svaṅgaḥ: One whose limbs are beautiful.

617. Śatānandaḥ: One who is non-dual and is of the nature of supreme bliss.

618. Nandiḥ: One who is of the nature of supreme Bliss.

619. Jyōtir-gaṇeśvaraḥ: One who is the Lord of the stars, that is, Jyotirgana.

620. Vijitātmā: One who has conquered the Atma that is the mind.

621. Vidheyātmā: One whose form or nature cannot be determined as 'only this'.

622. Satkīrtiḥ: One whose fame is of the nature of truth.

623. Chinna-saṁśayaḥ: One who has no doubts, as everything is clear to him like a fruit in the palm.

udīrṇaḥ sarvataścakṣuranīśaḥ śāśvatasthiraḥ, bhūśayō

bhūṣaṇō bhūtirviśōkaḥ śōkanāśanaḥ. (67)

624. Udīrṇaḥ: He who is superior to all beings.

625. Sarvataḥ-cakṣuḥ: One who, being of the nature of pure consciousness, can see everthing in all directions.

626. Anīśaḥ: One who cannot have anyone to lord over him.

627. Śāśvata-sthiraḥ: One, who though eternal is also unchanging.

628. Bhūśayaḥ: One who, while seeking the means to cross over to Lanka, had to sleep on the ground of the sea-beach.

629. Bhūṣaṇaḥ: One who adorned the earth by manifesting as various incarnations.

630. Bhūtiḥ: One who is the abode or the essence of everthing, or is the source of all glorious manifestations.

631. Viśōkaḥ: One who, being of the nature of bliss, is free from all sorrow.

632. Śōkanāśanaḥ: One who effaces the sorrows of devotees even by mere remembrance.

arciṣmānarcitaḥ kumbhō viśuddhātmā viśōdhanaḥ,

aniruddhōpratirathaḥ pradyumnōmitavikramaḥ. (68)

633. Arciṣmān: He by whose rays of light (Archish), the sun, the moon and other bodies are endowed with rays of light.

634. Arcitaḥ: One who is worshipped by Brahma and other Devas who are themselves the objects of worship in all the worlds.

635. Kumbhaḥ: He who contains in Himself everything as in a pot.

636. Viśuddhātmā: Being above the three Gunas, Satva, Rajas and Tamas, the Lord is pure spirit and is also free from all impurities.

637. Viśōdhanaḥ: One who destroys all sins by mere remembrance.

638. Aniruddhaḥ: The last one of the four Vyuhas – Vasudeva, Samkarshana, Pradyumna and Aniruddhaḥ. Or one who, cannot be obstructed by enemies.

639. Aprati-rathaḥ: One who has no Pratiratha or an equal antagonist to confront.

640. Pradyumnaḥ: One whose Dyumna or wealth is of a superior and sacred order. Or one of the four Vyuhas.

641. Amitavikramaḥ: One of unlimited prowess. Or one whose prowess cannot be obstructed by anyone.

kālaneminihā vīraḥ śauriḥ śūrajaneśvaraḥ, trilōkātmā

trilōkeśaḥ keśavaḥ keśihā hariḥ. (69)

642. Kālanemi-nihā: One who destroyed the Asura named Kalanemi.

643. Viraḥ: One who is courageous.

644. Śauriḥ: One who was born in the clan of Sura as Krishna.

645. Śūrajaneśvaraḥ: One who by his overwhelming prowess controls even great powers like Indra and others.

646. Trilōkātmā: One who in his capacity as the inner pervade is the soul for the three worlds.

647. Trilōkeśaḥ: One under whose guidance and command everything in the three words is functioning.

648. Keśavaḥ: By Kesha is meant the rays of light spreading within the orbit of the sun.

649. Keśihā: One who destroyed the Asura named Keshi.

650. Hariḥ: One who destroys Samsara, that is, entanglement in the cycle of birth and death along with ignorance, its cause.

kāmadevaḥ kāmapālaḥ kāmī kāntaḥ kṛtāgamaḥ,

anirdeśyavapurviṣṇurvīrōnantō dhanañjayaḥ. (70)

651. Kāmadevaḥ: One who is desired by persons in quest of the four values of life – Dharma, Artha, Kama and Moksha.

652. Kāmapālaḥ: One who protects or assures the desired ends of people endowed with desires.

653. Kāmī: One who by nature has all his desires satisfied.

654. Kāntaḥ: One whose form is endowed with great beauty. Or one who effects the 'Anta' or dissolution of 'Ka' or Brahma at the end of a Dviparardha (the period of Brahma's lifetime extending over a hundred divine years).

655. Kṛtāgamaḥ: He who produced scriptures like Shruti, Smruti and Agama.

656. Anirdeśya-vapuḥ: He is called so, because, being above the Gunas, His form cannot be determined.

657. Viṣṇuḥ: One whose brilliance has spread over the sky and over the earth.

658. Vīraḥ: One who has the power of Gati or movement.

659. Anantaḥ: One who pervades everything, who is eternal, who is the soul of all, and who cannot be limited by space, time, location, etc.

660. Dhananjayaḥ: Arjuna is called so because by his conquest of the kingdoms in the four quarters he acquired great wealth. Arjuna is a Vibhuti, a glorious manifestation of the Lord.

brahmaṇyō brahmakṛdbrahmā brahma brahmavivardhanaḥ,

brahmavidbrāhmaṇō brahmī brahmajñō brāhmaṇapriyaḥ. (71)

661. Brahmaṇyaḥ: The Vedas, Brahmanas and knowledge are indicated by the word Brahma. As the Lord promotes these, He is called Brahmanya.

662. Brahmakṛt: One who performs Brahma or Tapas (austerity).

663. Brahmā: One who creates everything as the creator Brahma.

664. Brahma: Being big expanding, the Lord who is known from indications like Satya (Truth), is called Brahma. Or Brahma is Truth, Knowledge and Infinity!

665. Brahma-vivardhanaḥ: One who promotes Tapas (austerity), etc.

666. Brahmavid: One who knows the Vedas and their real meaning.

667. Brāhmaṇaḥ: One who, in the form of Brahmana, instructs the whole world, saying, 'It is commanded so and so in the Veda'.

668. Brahmī: One in whom is established such entities as Tapas, Veda, mind, Prana etc. which are parts of Brahma and which are also called Brahma.

669. Brahmajñaḥ: One who knows the nature of Brahman.

670. Brāhmaṇapriyaḥ: One to whom holy men are devoted.

mahākramō mahākarmā mahātejā mahōragaḥ,

mahākraturmahāyajvā mahāyajñō mahāhaviḥ. (72)

671. Mahākramaḥ: One with enormous strides. May Vishnu with enormous strides bestow on us happiness.

672. Mahākarmā: One who is performing great works like the creation of the world.

673. Mahātejāḥ: He from whose brilliance, sun and other luminaries derive their brilliance. Or one who is endowed with the brilliance of various excellences.

674. Mahoragaḥ: He is also the great serpent.

675. Mahākratuḥ: He is the great Kratu or sacrifice.

676. Mahāyajvā: One who is great and performs sacrifices for the good of the world.

677. Mahāyajñaḥ: He who is the great sacrifice.

678. Mahāhaviḥ: The whole universe conceived as Brahman and offered as sacrificial offering (Havis) into the fire of the Self, which is Brahman.

stavyaḥ stavapriyaḥ stōtraṁ stutiḥ stōtā raṇapriyaḥ,

pūrṇaḥ pūrayitā puṇyaḥ puṇyakīrtiranāmayaḥ. (73)

679. Stavyaḥ: One who is the object of laudations of everyone but who never praises any other being.

680. Stava-priyaḥ: One who is pleased with hymns.

681. Stotraṁ: A Stotra means a hymn proclaiming the glory, attributes and names of the Lord.

682. Stutiḥ: A praise.

683. Stōtā: One who, being all -formed, is also the person who sings a hymn of praise.

684. Raṇapriyaḥ: One who is fond of fight for the protection of the world, and for the purpose always sports in His hands the five weapons, the discus Sudarshana, the mace Kaumodaki, the bow Saranga, and the sword Nandaka besides the conch Panchajanya.

685. Pūrṇaḥ: One who is self-fulfilled, being the source of all powers and excellences.

686. Pūrayitā: One who is not only self-fulfilled but gives all fulfillments to others.

687. Puṇyaḥ: One by only hearing about whom all sins are erased.

688. Puṇyakīrtiḥ: One of holy fame. His excellences are capable of conferring great merit on others.

689. Anāmayaḥ: One who is not afflicted by any disease that is born of cause, internal or external.

manōjavastīrthakarō vasuretā vasupradaḥ, vasupradō

vāsudevō vasurvasumanā haviḥ. (74)

690. Manōjavaḥ: One who, being all pervading, is said to be endowed with speed likes that of the mind.

691. Tīrthakaraḥ: Tirtha means Vidya, a particular branch of knowledge or skill.

692. Vasu-retāḥ: He whose Retas (Semen) is gold (Vasu).

693. Vasupradaḥ: One who gladly bestows wealth in abundance. He is really the master of all wealth, and others who seem to be so are in those positions only because of His grace.

694. Vasupradaḥ: One who bestows on devotees the highest of all wealth, namely Moksha.

695. Vāsudevaḥ: The son of Vasudeva.

696. Vasuḥ: He in whom all creation dwells.

697. Vasumanaḥ: One whose mind dwells equally in all things.

698. Haviḥ: Havis or sacrificial offerings.

sadgatiḥ satkṛtiḥ sattā sadbhūtiḥ satparāyaṇaḥ,

śūrasenō yaduśreṣṭhaḥ sannivāsaḥ suyāmunaḥ. (75)

699. Sadgatiḥ: One who is attained by such persons. Or who is endowed with intelligence of great excellence.

700. Satkṛtiḥ: One whose achievements are for the protection

of the world.

701. Sattā: Experience that is without any difference of an external nature from similar objects or dissimilar objects as also internal differences is called Satta.

702. Sad-bhūtiḥ: The Paramatman who is pure existence and conscousness, who is unsublatable and who manifests Himself in many ways.

703. Satparāyaṇaḥ: He who is the highest Status attainable by holy men who have realized the Truth.

704. Śūrasenaḥ: One having an army of heroic wariours like Hanuman.

705. Yaduśreṣṭhaḥ: One who is the greatest among the Yadus.

706. Sannivāsaḥ: One who is the resort of holy knowing ones.

707. Suyāmunaḥ: One who is surrounded by may illustrious persons associated with the river Yamuna like Devaki, Vasudeva, Nandagopa, Yasoda, Balabhadra, Subhadra, etc.

bhūtāvāsō vāsudevaḥ sarvāsunilayōnalaḥ,

darpahā darpadō dṛptō durdharōthāparājitaḥ. (76)

708. Bhūtāvāsaḥ: He in whom all the being's dwell.

709. Vāsudevaḥ: The Divinity who covers the whole universe by

Maya.

710. Sarvāsunilayaḥ: He in whose form as the Jiva all the vital energy or Prana of all living beings' dissolves.

711. Analaḥ: One whose wealth or power has no limits.

712. Darpahā: One who puts down the pride of persons who walk along the unrighteous path.

713. Darpadaḥ: One who endows those who walk the path of righteousness with a sense of self-respect regarding their way of life.

714. Dṛptaḥ: One who is ever satisfied by the enjoyment of His own inherent bliss.

715. Durdharaḥ: One who is very difficult to be borne or contained in the heart in meditation.

716. Aparājitaḥ: One who is never conquered by internal enemies like attachment and by external enemies like Asuras.

viśvamūrtirmahāmūrtirdīptamūrtiramūrtimān,

anekamūrtiravyaktaḥ śatamūrtiḥ śatānanaḥ. (77)

717. Viśvamūrtiḥ: One who, being the soul of all, has the whole universe as His body.

718. Mahāmūrtiḥ: One with an enormous form stretched on a bedstead constituted of the serpent Adisesha.

719. Dīptamūrtiḥ: One with a luminous form of knowledge.

720. Amūrtimān: He who is without a body born of Karma.

721. Anekamūrtiḥ: One who assumes several bodies in His incarnations as it pleases Him in or to help the world.

722. Avyaktaḥ: One who cannot be clearly described as 'This' even though He has many forms.

723. Śatamūrtiḥ: One who, though He is of the nature of Pure Consciousness, assumes different forms for temporary purposes.

724. Śatānanaḥ: He is called one with a hundred faces to indicate that He has several forms.

ekō naikaḥ savaḥ kaḥ kiṁ yattatpadamanuttamam,

lōkabandhurlōkanāthō mādhavō bhaktavatsalaḥ. (78)

725. Ekaḥ: One without any kind of differences that are internal or that relate to similar objects external or to dissimilar objects.

726. Naikaḥ: One who has numerous bodies born of Maya.

727. Savaḥ: That Yajna in which Soma is made.

728. Kaḥ: The syllable 'Ka' indicates joy or happiness. So, it means one who is hymned as constituted of joy.

729. Kim: One who is fit to be contemplated upon, because He is the summation of all values.

730. Yat: One who is by nature existent. The word 'Yat' indicates a self-subsisting entity.

731. Tat: Brahma is so called because He 'expands'.

732. Padamanuttamam: Braman is 'Pada' or Status, because He is the goal of all Moksha-seekers. It is Anuttama, because It is that beyond which there is nothing else to be attained.

733. Lokabandhuḥ: One who is friend of the world.

734. Lokanāthah: One to whom all the worlds pray.

735. Mādhavaḥ: One who was born in the clan of Madhu.

736. Bhaktavatsalaḥ: One who has got love for devotees.

suvarṇavarṇō hemāṅgō varāṅgaścandanāṅgadī, vīrahā

viṣamaḥ śūnyō ghṛtāśīracalaścalaḥ. (79)

737. Suvarṇavarṇaḥ: One who has got the colour of gold.

738. Hemāṅgaḥ: One whose form is like that of gold.

739. Varāṅgaḥ: He the parts of whose form are brilliant.

740. Candanāṅgadī: One who is adorned with armlets that generate joy.

741. Vīrahā: One who destroyed heroes (Viras) like Kiranyakashipu for protecting Dharma.

742. Viṣamaḥ: One to whom there is no euql because nothing is comparable to Him by any characteristic.

743. Śūnyaḥ: One who, being without any attributes, appears as Sunya (emptiness).

744. Ghṛtāśīḥ: One whose blessings are unfailing.

745. Acalaḥ: One who cannot be deprived of His real nature as Truth, Intelligence and Infinity.

746. Calaḥ: One who moves in the form of air.

amānī mānadō mānyō lōkasvāmī trilōkadhṛt,

sumedhā medhajō dhanyaḥ satyamedhā dharādharaḥ. (80)

747. Amānī: He who, being of the nature of Pure Consciousness, has no sense of identification with anything that is not Atman.

748. Mānadaḥ: One who by His power of Maya induces the sense of self in non-self. Or one who has regard and beneficence towards devotees. Or one who destroys in the knowing ones the sense of identification with the non-self.

749. Mānyaḥ: One who is to be adored by all, because He is the God of all.

750. Lokasvāmī: One who is the Lord of all the fourteen spheres.

751. Trilokadhṛt: One who supports all the three worlds.

752. Sumedhāḥ: One with great and beneficent intelligence.

753. Medhajaḥ: One who arose from Yaga (a kind of sacrifice).

754. Dhanyaḥ: One who has attained all His ends and therefore is self-satisfied.

755. Satyamedhāḥ: One whose intelligence is fruitful.

756. Dharādharaḥ: The One Who Holds and Supports the Earth.

tejōvṛṣō dyutidharaḥ sarvaśastrabhṛtāṁ varaḥ,

pragrahō nigrahō vyagrō naikaśṛṅgō gadāgrajaḥ. (81)

757. Tejōvṛṣaḥ: One who in the form of the sun causes rainfall at all times.

758. Dyutidharaḥ: One whose form is always brilliant.

759. Sarva-śastra-bhṛtāṁ varaḥ: One who is superior to all bearing arms.

760. Pragrahaḥ: One who accepts the offerings of devotees with great delight.

761. Nigrahaḥ: One who controls and destroys everything.

762. Vyagraḥ: One who has no Agra or end. Or one who is very attentive (Vyagra) in granting the prayers of devotees.

763. Naikaśṛṅgaḥ: One with four horns.

764. Gadāgrajaḥ: One who is revealed first by Mantra (Nigada). Or one who is the elder brother of Gada.

caturmūrtiścaturbāhuścaturvyūhaścaturgatiḥ, caturātmā

caturbhāvaścaturvedavidekapāt. (82)

765. Caturmūrtiḥ: One with four aspects as Virat, Sutratma, Avyakruta, and Turiya. Or one with four horns with colours white, red, yellow and black.

766. Caturbāhuḥ: One with four arms, as Vasudeva is always described.

767. Caturvyūhaḥ: One having four manifestations.

768. Caturgatiḥ: One who is sought as the end by the four Orders of life and four Varnas ordained by the scriptures.

769. Caturātmā: One whose self is specially endowed with puissance, because it is without any attachment, antagonism, etc.

770. Caturbhāvaḥ: One from whom has originated the four human values - Dharma, Artha, Kama, and Moksha.

771. Catur-vedavid: One who understands the true meaning of the four Vedas.

772. Ekapāt: One with a single Pada, part or leg. Or one with a single foot or manifestation.

samāvartō nivṛttātmā durjayō duratikramaḥ, durlabhō

durgamō durgō durāvāsō durārihā. (83)

773. Samāvartaḥ: One who effectively whirls the wheel

of Samsara.

774. Anivrutātmā: One who is not Nivruta (separated from) anything or anywhere, because He is all-pervading.

775. Durjayaḥ: One who cannot be conquered.

776. Duratikramaḥ: One out of fear of whom, even heavenly objects like sun do not dare to oppose His command.

777. Durlabhaḥ: One who can be attained by Bhakti, which is difficult for a person to be endowed with.

778. Durgamaḥ: One whom it is difficult to attain.

779. Durgaḥ: One the attainment of whom is rendered difficult by various obstructions.

780. Durāvāsaḥ: He whom the Yogis with very great difficulty bring to reside in their hearts in Samadhi.

781. Durārihā: One who destroys beings like Asuras.

śubhāṅgō lōkasāraṅgaḥ sutantustantuvardhanaḥ,

indrakarmā mahākarmā kṛtakarmā kṛtāgamaḥ. (84)

782. Śubhāṅgaḥ: One whose form is very auspicious to meditate upon.

783. Lōkasāraṅgaḥ: One who like the Saranga (honey-beetle) grasps the essence of the world.

784. Sutantuḥ: As this universe of infinite extension belongs to Him, the Lord is called Sutantu.

785. Tantu-vardhanaḥ: One who can augment or contract the web of this world.

786. Indra-karmā: One whose actions are like that of Indra, that is, are of a highly commendable nature.

787. Mahākarmā: One of whom the great elements like Akasha are effects.

788. Kṛtakarmā: One who has fulfilled everything and has nothing more to accomplish.

789. Kṛtāgamaḥ: One who has given out the Agama in the shape of the Veda.

udbhavaḥ sundaraḥ sundō ratnanābhaḥ sulōcanaḥ, arkō

vājasanaḥ śṛṅgī jayantaḥ sarvavijjayī . (85)

790. Udbhavaḥ: One who assumes great and noble embodiments out of His own will.

791. Sundaraḥ: One who has a graceful attractiveness that surprises everyone.

792. Sundaḥ: One who is noted for extreme tenderness (Undanam).

793. Ratna-nābhaḥ: Ratna indicates beauty; so one whose navel is very beautiful.

794. Sulōcanaḥ: One who has brilliant eyes, that is, knowledge of everything.

795. Arkaḥ: One who is being worshipped even by beings like Brahma who are themselves objects of worship.

796. Vājasanaḥ: One who gives Vajam (food) to those who entreat Him.

797. Śṛṅgī: One who at the time of Pralaya (cosmic dissolution) assumed the form of a fish having prominent antenna.

798. Jayantaḥ: One who conquers enemies easily.

799. Sarvavijjayī: The Lord is 'Sarvavit' as He has knowledge of everything. He is 'Jayi' because He is the conqueror of all the inner forces like attachment, anger etc., as also of external foes like Hiranyaksha.

suvarṇabindurakṣōbhyaḥ sarvavāgīśvareśvaraḥ,

mahāhradō mahāgartō mahābhūtō mahānidhiḥ. (86)

800. Suvarṇabinduḥ: One whose 'Bindus' that is, limbs, are euaql to gold in brilliance.

801. Akṣobhyaḥ: One who is never perturbed by passions like attachment and aversion, by objects of the senses like sound, taste, etc., and by Asuras the antagonists of the Devas.

802. Sarva-vāgīśvareśvaraḥ: One who is the master of all masters of learning, including Brahma.

803. Mahāhradaḥ: He is called a great Hrada (lake), because being the paramatman who is of the nature of Bliss, the Yogis who contemplate upon Him dip themselves in that lake of Bliss and attain to great joy.

804. Mahāgartaḥ: One whose Maya is difficult to cross like a big pit.

805. Mahābhūtaḥ: One who is not divided by the three periods of time – past, present and future.

806. Mahānidhiḥ: One in whom all the great elements have their support. He is Mahan or a great one and 'Nidhi', the most precious one.

kumudaḥ kundaraḥ kundaḥ parjanyaḥ pāvano'nilaḥ,

amṛtāśōmṛtavapuḥ sarvajñaḥ sarvatōmukhaḥ. (87)

807. Kumudaḥ: 'Ku' means earth; one who gives joy (muda) to the earth by freeing it of its burdens is Kumuda.

808. Kundaraḥ: One who offers blessings as pure as Kunda or jasmine.

809. Kundaḥ: One who has limbs as beautiful as Kunda or Jasmine.

810. Parjanyaḥ: The word means cloud. One who resembles the cloud in extinguishing the three Tapas (heats, that is, miseries) arising from psychological, material and spiritual causes. Or one who rains all desires like a cloud.

811. Pāvanaḥ: One by merely remembering whom a devotee attains purity.

812. Anilaḥ: 'Ilanam' means inducement. One who is without any inducement is Anila. Ilana also means sleep. So one who sleeps not or is ever awake is Anila.

813. Amṛtāśaḥ: One who consumes Amruta or immortal bliss, which is His own nature.

814. Amṛtavapuḥ: One whose form is deathless, that is, undecaying.

815. Sarvajñaḥ: One who is all-knowing.

816. Sarvatōmukhaḥ: One who has faces everywhere.

sulabhaḥ suvrataḥ siddhaḥ śatrujicchatrutāpanaḥ,

nyagrodho'dumbaro'śvatthaścāṇūrāndhraniṣūdanaḥ. (88)

817. Sulabhaḥ: One who is attained easily by offering trifles like leaf, flower, and fruits etc., with devotion.

818. Suvrataḥ: 'Vratati' means enjoys. So, one who enjoys pure offerings. It can also mean one who is a non-enjoyer, that is, a mere witness.

819. Siddhaḥ: One whose objects are always attained, that is, omnipotent and unobstructed by any other will.

820. Śatrujit: Conqueror of all forces of evil.

821. Śatrutāpanaḥ: One who destroys the enemies of the Devas.

822. Nyagrodhaḥ: That which remains above all and grows downward. That is, He is the source of everything that is manifest.

823. Udumbaraḥ: One who as the Supreme cause is 'above the sky', that is, superior to all.

824. Aśvatthaḥ: That which does not last even for the next day.

825. Cāṇūrāndhra-niṣūdanaḥ: One who destroyed a valiant fighter Chanura belonging to the race of Andhra.

sahasrārciḥ saptajihvaḥ saptaidhāḥ saptavāhanaḥ,

amūrtiranaghōcintyō bhayakṛdbhayanāśanaḥ. (89)

826. Sahasrārciḥ: One with innumerable Archis or rays.

827. Sapta-jihvaḥ: The Lord in his manifestation as Fire is conceived as having seven tongues of flame.

828. Saptaidhāḥ: The Lord who is of the nature of fire has seven Edhas or forms of brilliance.

829. Saptavāhanaḥ: The Lord in the form of Surya or sun has seven horses as his vehicles or mounts.

830. Amūrtiḥ: One who is without sins or without sorrow.

831. Achintyo: One who is not determinable by any criteria of knowledge, being Himself the witnessing Self- certifying all knowledge.

832. Anaghaḥ: One who is without sins or without sorrow.

833. Bhayakṛud: One who generates fear in those who go along the evil path. Or one who cuts at the root of all fear.

834. Bhaya-nāśanaḥ: One who destroys the fears of the virtuous.

aṇurbṛhatkṛśaḥ sthūlō guṇabhṛnnirguṇō mahān,|

adhṛtassvadhṛtasvāsyaḥ prāgvaṁśō vaṁśavardhanaḥ. (90)

835. Aṇuḥ: One who is extremely subtle.

836. Bṛhat: The huge and mighty.

837. Kṛśaḥ: One who is non-material.

838. Sthūlaḥ: Being the inner pervader of all, He is figuratively described as Stula or huge.

839. Guṇa-bhṛt: The support of the Gunas. He is so called because in the creative cycle of creation, sustentation, and dissolution, He is the support of the Gunas – Satva, Rajas and Tamas – with which these functions are performed.

840. Nirguṇaḥ: One who is without the Gunas of Prakruti.

841. Mahān: The great.

842. Adhṛutaḥ: One who, being the support of all supporting agencies, like Pruthvi (Earth), is not supported by anything external to Him.

843. Svadhṛtaḥ: One supported by oneself.

844. Svāsyaḥ: One whose face is beautiful and slightly red like the inside of a lotus flower.

845. Prāgvaṁśaḥ: The family lines of others are preceded by the lines of still others, but the Lord's descendent, namely, the world system, is not preceded by anything else.

846. Vaṁśavardhanaḥ: One who augments or destroys the world-system, which is His off-spring.

bhārabhṛt kathitō yōgī yōgīśaḥ sarvakāmadaḥ,

āśramaḥ śramaṇaḥ, kṣāmaḥ suparṇō vāyuvāhanaḥ. (91)

847. Bhārabhṛt: One who bears the weight of the earth assuming the form of Ananta.

848. Kathitaḥ: One who is spoken of as the highest by the Veda or one of whom all Vedas speak.

849. Yogī: Yoga here means knowledge. So He who is attained by that is Yogi. Or Yoga means Samadhi. He who is ever established in His own Self, that is, the Paramatma. He is therefore Yogi.

850. Yogīśaḥ: He who is never shaken from Yoga or knowledge and establishment in His own Self, unlike ordinary Yogis who slip away from Yoga on account of obstacles.

851. Sarva-kāmadaḥ: One who bestows all desired fruits.

852. Āśramaḥ: One who is the bestower of rest on all who are wandering in the forest of Samsara.

853. Śramaṇaḥ: One who brings tribulations to those who live without using their discriminative power.

854. Kṣāmaḥ: He who brings about the decline of all beings.

855. Suparṇaḥ: The lord who has manifested Himself as the tree

of Samsara has excellent leaves (Parna) in the form of Vedic passages (Chandas).

856. Vāyuvāhanaḥ: He for fear of whom Vayu (Air) carries all beings.

dhanurdharō dhanurvedō daṅḍō damayitā damaḥ,

aparājitassarvasahō niyantā niyamō yamaḥ. (92)

857. Dhanurdharaḥ: He who as Rama wielded the great bow.

858. Dhanurvedaḥ: He who as the same Rama, the son of Dasharatha, was the master of the science of archery.

859. Daṅḍaḥ: He who is discipline among the disciplinarians.

860. Damayitā: He who inflicts punishments on people as Yama and as king.

861. Damaḥ: He who is in the form of self-descipline in men as a result of enforcement.

862. Aparājitaḥ: One who is never defeated by enemies.

863. Sarvasahaḥ: One who is expert in all Karmas (works).

864. Niyantā: One who appoints every person to his respective duties.

865. Aniyamaḥ: One on whom there is no enforcement of any law, or above whom there can be no overlord to enforce anything, as He is the controller of everything.

866. Ayamaḥ: One on whom Yama has no control, that is one who has no death.

sattvavān sāttvikaḥ satyaḥ satyadharmaparāyaṇaḥ,

abhiprāyaḥ priyārho'rhaḥ priyakṛt pritivardhanaḥ. (93)

867. Satvavān: One who has got the strengthening qualities like heroism, prowess, etc.

868. Sāttvikaḥ: One who is established essentially in the Satva Guna.

869. Satyaḥ: One who is truly established in good people.

870. Satya-dharma-parāyaṇaḥ: One who is present in truthfulness

and righteousness in its many aspects.

871. Abhiprāyaḥ: The One who is sought after by those who seek the ultimate values of life (Purushartha).

872. Priyārhaḥ: The being to whom the objects that are dear to oneself, are fit to be offered.

873. Arhaḥ: One who deserves to be worshipped with all the ingredients and rites of worship like offerings, praise, prostration, etc.

874. Priyakṛt: One who is not only to be loved but who does what is good and dear to those who worship Him.

875. Pritivardhanaḥ: One who enhances the joys of devotees.

vihāyasagatirjyōtiḥ surucirhutabhugvibhuḥ,

ravirvirōcanaḥ sūryaḥ savitā ravilōcanaḥ. (94)

876. Vihāyasa-gatiḥ: One who is the support of Vishupada.

877. Jyotiḥ: One who is the light of self-luminous consciousness that reveals oneself as well as other things.

878. Suruciḥ: The Lord whose Ruchi i.e. brilliance or will, is of an attractive nature.

879. Hutabhuk: One who eats, that is, receives, whatever is offered to whatever deities (Devas) in all sacrifices.

880. Vibhuḥ: One who dwells everywhere. Or one who is the master of all the three worlds.

881. Raviḥ: One who absorbs all Rasas (fluids) in the form of the Sun.

882. Virōcanaḥ: One who shines in many ways.

883. Sūryaḥ: One who generates Shri or brilliance in Surya. Or Agni (Fire) is what is called Surya.

884. Savitā: One who brings forth (Prasava) all the worlds.

885. Ravi-lōcanaḥ: One having the sun as the eye.

anantō hutabhugbhōktā sukhadō naikajōgrajaḥ,

anirviṇṇaḥ sadāmarṣī lōkādhiṣṭhānamadbhutaḥ. (95)

886. Anantaḥ: One who is eternal, all-pervading and indeterminable by space and time.

887. Hutabhuk: One who consumes what is offered in fire sacrifices.

888. Bhoktā: One to whom the unconscious Prakruti is the object for enjoyment.

889. Sukhadaḥ: One who bestows liberation (Miksha) on devotees.

890. Naikajaḥ: One who takes on birth again and again for the preservation of Dharma.

891. Agrajaḥ: One who was born before everything else, that is, Hiranyagarbha.

892. Anirviṇṇaḥ: One who is free from all sorrow, because he has secured all his desires and has no obstruction in the way of such achievement.

893. Sadāmarṣī: One who is always patient towards good men.

894. Lōkādhiṣṭhānam: Brahman who, though without any other support for Himself, supports all the three worlds.

895. Adbhutaḥ: The wonderful being.

sanātsanātanatamaḥ kapilaḥ kapiravyayaḥ,

svastidaḥ svastikṛtsvasti svastibhuksvastidakṣiṇaḥ. (96)

896. Sanāt: The word Sanat indicates a great length of time. Time also is the manifestation of the Supreme Being.

897. Sanātanatamaḥ: Being the cause of all, He is more ancient than Brahma and other beings, who are generally considered eternal.

898. Kapilaḥ: A subterranean fire in the ocean is Kapila, light red in colour.

899. Kapiḥ: 'Ka' means water. One who drinks or absorbs all water by his Kapi, that is, the sun.

900. Avyayaḥ: One in whom all the worlds get dissolved in Pralaya.

901. Svastidaḥ: One who gives what is auspicious to devotees.

902. Svastikṛt: One who works bestowing what is good.

903. Svasti: One whose auspicious form is characterized by supreme Bliss.

904. Svastibhuk: One who enjoys the Svasti mentioned above or who preserves the Svasti of devotees.

905. Svastidakṣiṇaḥ: One who augments as Svasti (auspiciousness).

araudraḥ kuṇḍalī cakrī vikramyūrjitaśāsanaḥ, śabdātigaḥ

śabdasahaḥ śiśiraḥ śarvarīkaraḥ. (97)

906. Araudraḥ: Action, attachment and anger these three are Raudra. The Lord is one whose desires are all accomplished, so He has no attachment or aversion. So He is free from the Raudras mentioned above.

907. Kuṇḍalī: One who has taken the form of Adisesha.

908. Cakrī: One who sports in his hand the discus named Sudarshana, which is the category known as Manas, for the protection of all the worlds.

909. Vikramī: Vikrama means taking a stride, as also courage.

910. Ūrjita-śāsanaḥ: One whose dictates in the form of shrutis and smrutis are of an extremely sublime nature.

911. Śabdātigaḥ: One who cannot be denoted by any sound because He has none of the characteristics, which could be grasped by sound.

912. Śabdasahaḥ: One who is the purport of all Vedas.

913. Śiśiraḥ: One who is the shelter to those who are bruning in the three types of wordly fires – sufferings arising from material causes, psychological causes and spiritual causes.

914. Śarvarīkaraḥ: For those in bondage, the Atman is like Sarvari (night) and for an enlightened one the state of samsara is like night (Sarvari). So the Lord is called the one who generates Sarvari or night for both the enlightened and the bound ones.

akrūraḥ peśalō dakṣō dakṣiṇaḥ, kṣamiṇāṁ varaḥ,

vidvattamō vītabhayaḥ puṇyaśravaṇakīrtanaḥ. (98)

915. Akrūraḥ: One who is without cruelty.

916. Peśalaḥ: One who is handsome in regard to His actions, mind, word and body.

917. Dakṣaḥ: One who is full-grown, strong and does everything quickly, such a person is Daksha.

918. Dakṣiṇaḥ: This word is also means the same as the above Nama.

919. Kṣamiṇāṁ varaḥ: The greatest among the patient ones, because He is more patient than all Yogis noted for patience.

920. Vidvattamaḥ: He who has got the unsurpassable and all-inclusive knowledge of everything.

921. Vītabhayaḥ: One who, being eternally free and the Lord of all, is free from the fear of transmigratory life.

922. Puṇya-śravaṇa-kīrtanaḥ: One to hear about whom and to sing of whom is meritorious.

uttāraṇō duṣkṛtihā puṇyō duḥsvapnanāśanaḥ,

vīrahā rakṣaṇassantō jīvanaḥ paryavasthitaḥ. (99)

923. Uttāraṇaḥ: One who takes beings over to the other shore of the ocean of Samsara.

924. Duṣkṛtihā: One who effaces the evil effects of evil actions. Or one who destroys those who perform evil.

925. Puṇyaḥ: One who bestows holiness on those who remember and adore Him.

926. Duḥsvapna-nāśanaḥ: When adored and meditated upon, He saves one from dreams foreboding danger. Hence He is called so.

927. Vīrahā: One who frees Jivas from bondage and thus saves them from the various transmigratory paths by bestowing liberation on them.

928. Rakṣaṇaḥ: One who, assuming the Satvaguna, protects all the three worlds.

929. Santaḥ: Those who adopt the virtuous path are called good men (Santah).

930. Jīvanaḥ: One who supports the lives of all beings as Prana.

931. Paryavasthitaḥ: One who remains pervading everywhere in this universe.

anantarūpōnantaśrīrjitamanyurbhayāpahaḥ, caturaśrō

gabhīrātmā vidiśō vyādiśō diśaḥ. (100)

932. Ananta-rūpaḥ: One who has innumerable forms, as He dwells in this all-comprehending universe.

933. Anantaśrīḥ: One whose Shri (glory) is infinite.

934. Jita-manyuḥ: One who has overcome anger.

935. Bhayāpahaḥ: One who destroys the fears of beings from Samsara.

936. Caturaśraḥ: One who is just, because He bestows on Jivas the fruits of their Karma.

937. Gabhirātmā: One whose nature is unfathomable.

938. Vidiśaḥ: One who distributes various furits of actions to persons differing in their forms according to competency.

939. Vyādiśaḥ: One who gives to Indra and other deities directions according to their varied functions.

940. Diśaḥ: One who in the form of the Vedas bestows the fruits of their ritualistic actions on different beings.

anādirbhūrbhuvō lakṣmīssuvīrō rucirāṅgadaḥ,

jananō janajanmādirbhīmō bhīmaparākramaḥ. (101)

941. Anādiḥ: One who has no beginning because He is the ultimate

cause of all.

942. Bhūrbhuvaḥ: 'Bhu' means support. One who is the support (Bhu) of even the earth, which is known to support all things.

943. Lakṣmiḥ: He who is the bestower of all that is auspicious to the earth besides being its supporter.

944. Suvīraḥ: One who has many brilliant ways of manifestation.

945. Ruchirāṅgadaḥ: One who has very attractive armlets.

946. Jananaḥ: One who gives brith to living beings.

947. Jana-janmādiḥ: One who is the root cause of the origin of Jivas that come to have embodiment.

948. Bhimaḥ: One who is the cause of fear.

949. Bhima-parākramaḥ: One whose power and courage in His incarnations were a cause of fear for the Asuras.

ādhāranilayōdhātā puṣpahāsaḥ prajāgaraḥ,

ūrdhvagassatpathācāraḥ prāṇadaḥ praṇavaḥ paṇaḥ. (102)

950. Ādhāra-nilayaḥ: One who is the support of even all the basic supporting factors like the five elements – Ether, Air, Fire, Water and Earth.

951. Adhātā: One who is one's own support and therefore does not require another support.

952. Puṣpahāsaḥ: One whose manifestation as the universe

resembles the Hasa or blooming of buds into flowers.

953. Prajāgaraḥ: One who is particularly awake, because He is eternal Awareness.

954. Ūrdhvagaḥ: One who is above everything.

955. Satpathācāraḥ: One who follows the conduct of the good.

956. Prāṇadaḥ: One who givesback life to dead ones as in the case of Parikshit.

957. Praṇavaḥ: Pranava (Om) the manifesting sound symbol

of Brahman. As He is inseparably related with Pranava, He is called Pranava.

958. Paṇaḥ: It comes from the root 'Prana' meaning transaction. So, one who bestows the fruits of Karma on all according to their Karma.

pramāṇaṁ prāṇanilayaḥ prāṇabhṛt prāṇajīvanaḥ, tattvaṁ

tattvavidekātmā janmamṛtyujarātigaḥ. (103)

959. Pramāṇaṁ: One who is self-certifying, as He is Pure Consciousness.

960. Prāṇanilayaḥ: The home or dissolving ground of the Pranas.

961. Prāṇa-bhṛt: One who strengthens the Pranas as food (Anna).

962. Prāṇa-jīvanaḥ: He who keeps alive human beings with Vayus (airs) known as Prana, Apana etc.

963. Tattvaṁ: Means Brahman, just as words like Amruta, Satya, Paramartha, etc.

964. Tatvavid: One who knowns His own true nature.

965. Ekātmā: One who is the sole being and the spirit (Atma) in all.

966. Janma-mṛtyu-jarātigaḥ: One who subsists without being subject to the six kinds of transformations – being born, existing, temporarily, growing, transforming, decaying and dying.

bhūrbhuvaḥsvastarustāraḥ savitā prapitāmahaḥ, yajñō

yajñapatiryajvā yajñāṅgō yajñavāhanaḥ. (104)

967. Bhūr-bhuvaḥ-svastaruḥ: The three Vyahrutis Bhuh, Bhuvah, Svah are said to be the essence of the Veda.

968. Tāraḥ: One who helps Jivas to go across the ocean of Samsara.

969. Savitā: He who generates all the worlds.

970. Prapitāmahaḥ: One who is the father of Brahma and therefore the grandfather of all.

971. Yajñaḥ: One who is of the form of Yajna.

972. Yajñapatiḥ: One who is the protector and the master of the Yajnas.

973. Yajvā: One who manifests as the performer of a Yajna.

974. Yajñāngaḥ: All the parts of His body as the incarnate Cosmic Boar are identified with the parts of a yajna.

975. Yajña-vāhanaḥ: One who supports the Yajna which yield various fruits.

yajñabhṛdyajñakṛdyajñī yajñabhugyajñasādhanaḥ,

yajñāntakṛdyajñaguhyamannamannāda eva ca. (105)

976. Yajñabhṛd: He is so called, because He is the protector and supporter of all Yajna.

977. Yajñakṛd: One who performs Yajna at the beginnig and end of the world.

978. Yajñi: One who is the principal.

979. Yajñabhug: One who is the enjoyer of Yajna or Protector of Yajna.

980. Yajña-sādhanaḥ: One to whom the Yagya is the approach.

981. Yajñāntakṛd: One who is the end or the fruits of Yajna.

982. Yayajñaguhyam: The Gyana Yajna or the sacrifice of knowledge, which is the esoteric (Guhyam) of all the Yajnams.

983. Annam: That which is eaten by living beings. Or He who eats all beings.

984. Annādaḥ: One who is the eater of the whole world as food. The word Eva is added to show that He is also Anna, the food eaten.

ātmayōniḥ svayaṁjātō vaikhānaḥ sāmagāyanaḥ,

devakīnandanaḥ sraṣṭā kṣitīśaḥ pāpanāśanaḥ. (106)

985. Ātmayōniḥ: One who is the source of all; that is, there is no material cause other than Himself for the universe.

986. Svayaṁ-jātaḥ: He is also the instrumental cause.

987. Vaikhānaḥ: One who excavated the earth, taking a unique form.

988. Sāmagāyanaḥ: One who recites the Sama chants.

989. Devakī-nandanaḥ: The Son of Devaki in the incarnation as Krishna.

990. Sraṣṭā: The creator of all the worlds.

991. Kṣitīśaḥ: A master of the world. Here it denotes Rama.

992. Pāpanāśanaḥ: He who destroys the sins of those who adore Him, meditate upon Him, remember and sing hymns of praise on Him.

śaṅkhabhṛnnandakī cakrī śārṅgadhanvā gadādharaḥ,

rathāṅgapāṇirakṣōbhyaḥ sarvapraharaṇāyudhaḥ. sarvapraharaṇāyudha

oṃ nama iti. (107)

993. Śaṅkhabhṛt: One who sports the conch known as

Panchajanya, which stands for Tamasahamkara, of which the five elements are born.

994. Nandakī: One who has in His hand the sword known as Nandaka, which stands for Vidya (spiritual illumination).

995. Cakri: One who sports the discus known as Sudarshana, which stands for the Rajasahamkara, out of which the Indriyas have come.

996. Śārṅga-dhanvā: One who aims His Sarnga bow.

997. Gadādharaḥ: One who has the mace known as the Kaumodaki, which stands for the category of Buddhi.

998. Rathāṅga-pāṇiḥ: One in whose hand is a wheel (Chakra).

999. Akṣobhyaḥ: One who cannot be upset by anything, because He controls all the above-mentioned weapons.

1000. Sarva-praharaṇā-yudhaḥ: There is no rule that the Lord has got only the above- mentioned weapons. All things, which can be used for contacting or striking, are His weapons.

vanamālī gadī śārṅgī śaṅkhī cakrī ca nandakī, śrīmān nārāyaṇō

viṣṇurvāsudevōbhirakṣatu. (108) śrī vāsudevo'bhirakṣatu oṃ nama iti.

(Chant this shloka 3 times)

Protect us Oh Lord Narayana Who wears the forest garland,

Who has the mace, conch, sword and the wheel. And who is called Vishnu and the Vasudeva.

CHAPTER 3. PHALASHRUTI (VERSES OF BENEFITS)

Benefits:

The **Uttaranyasa verses (1-26)** of the *Vishnu Sahasranama* beautifully summarize the **benefits and divine power** of reciting or listening to the thousand names of Lord Vishnu. Here's a concise summary of the **key benefits** mentioned in these verses:

Spiritual Benefits

- **Liberation from sins**: Reciting the names purifies the soul and removes all sins (verse 10).
- **Freedom from rebirth**: Devotees are not subjected to the cycles of birth and death (verse 11).
- **Attainment of Moksha**: Leads to the realization of Brahman, or the Supreme Truth (verse 10).
- **Inner purity**: Cultivates qualities like peace, self-control, memory, fame, and devotion (verses 12-13).

Mental and Emotional Well-being

- **Freedom from fear, anxiety, anger, jealousy, and greed** (verses 7, 13).
- **Mental strength and clarity**: Increases inner power and resilience (verse 7).

Material and Social Gains

- **Fulfills desires**: Including dharma (righteousness), artha (wealth), kama (desires), and praja (progeny) (verse 4).
- **Success in one's duties**: Brāhmaṇas gain wisdom, Kṣatriyas victory, Vaiśyas wealth, and Śūdras comfort (verse 3).
- **Fame, fortune, and leadership**: Brings social prestige and prosperity (verse 6).

Health and Protection

- **Healing from illness**: Removes diseases and suffering (verse 8).
- **Freedom from bondage**: Both physical (prison) and mental (fears) (verse 8).
- **Safety through adversities**: Helps overcome all difficulties (verse 9).

Universal Perspective

- Everything—gods, nature, humans, knowledge—originates from and is governed by **Vasudeva (Krishna)** (verses 14–20).
- Reciting these names is as effective as engaging in other spiritual practices like yoga, jñāna (knowledge), or scriptural study (verse 19).

Practical Wisdom

- Even **one shloka** sincerely recited is sufficient to please the Lord (verse 24).
- Simple, heartfelt devotion is more important than elaborate rituals (verses 24–26).

Uttaranyasa Verses 1–26: English Transliteration and Simple Meaning

bhīṣma uvāca —

itīdaṁ kīrtanīyasya keśavasya mahātmanaḥ,

nāmnāṁ sahasraṁ divyānām aśeṣeṇa prakīrtitam||1||.

Bhishma said: Thus, is sung the thousand divine names of the great soul, Keshava.

ya idaṁ śṛṇuyānnityaṁ yaścāpi parikīrtayet,

nāśubhaṁ prāpnuyāt kiñcit somutreha ca mānavaḥ.||2||

One who hears or recites this daily will never face anything inauspicious in this life or the next.

vedāntagō brāhmaṇaḥ syāt kṣatriyo vijayī bhavet,

vaiśyo dhanasamṛddhaḥ syācchūdraḥ sukhamavāpnuyāt||3||.

The Brahmin gains knowledge, the Kshatriya wins victory, the Vaishya attains wealth, and the Shudra gains comfort.

dharmārthī prāpnuyād dharmaṁ arthārthī cārtham āpnuyāt,

kāmān avāpnuyāt kāmī prajārthī prāpnuyāt prajām||4||.

One desiring righteousness gains dharma, wealth-seekers gain wealth, desire-seekers fulfill desires, and those wishing for children are blessed.

bhaktimān yaḥ sadotthāya śucis tadgatamānasaḥ,

sahasraṁ vāsudevasya nāmnām etat prakīrtayet||5||.

A devoted, pure person who rises early and concentrates on the Lord will recite these thousand names.

yaśaḥ prāpnōti vipulaṁ yāti prādhānyam eva ca,

acalāṁ śriyam āpnōti śreyaḥ prāpnōty anuttamam.||6||

Such a person gains fame, leadership, stable wealth, and the highest good.

na bhayaṁ kvacid āpnōti vīryaṁ tejaś ca vindati,

bhavaty arōgō dyutimān bala-rūpa-guṇānvitaḥ.||7||

He becomes fearless, healthy, radiant, strong, and virtuous.

rōgārtō mucyate rōgād baddhō mucyeta bandhanāt,

bhayān mucyeta bhītas tu mucyeta āpadaḥ.||8||

The sick is cured, the imprisoned are freed, the fearful lose fear, and the troubled are rescued.

durgāṇy atitaraty āśu puruṣaḥ puruṣōttamam,

stuvannāma-sahasreṇa nityaṁ bhakti-samanvitaḥ.||9||

A person overcome with devotion easily crosses hardships by daily chanting the thousand names of the Supreme Lord.

vāsudevāśrayō martyo vāsudeva-parāyaṇaḥ,

sarvapāpa-viśuddhātmā yāti brahma sanātanam.||10||

The one who surrenders to Vasudeva and stays devoted is freed from all sins and reaches eternal Brahman.

na vāsudeva-bhaktānām aśubhaṁ vidyate kvacit,

janma-mṛtyu-jarā-vyādhi-bhayaṁ naiva upajāyate||11||.

Devotees of Vasudeva never face misfortune or fear of birth, death, aging, or illness.

imaṁ stavam adhīyānaḥ śraddhā-bhakti-samanvitaḥ,

yujyetātmā sukha-kṣānti-śrī-dhṛti-smṛti-kīrtibhiḥ||12||.

One who studies this with faith and devotion gains peace, happiness, wealth, patience, memory, and fame.

na krōdhō na ca mātsaryaṁ na lōbhō nāśubhā matiḥ,

bhavanti kṛtapuṇyānāṁ bhaktānāṁ puruṣōttame.||13||

Devotees of the Supreme Lord are free from anger, jealousy, greed, and wicked thoughts.

dyaussacandrārkanakṣatrā khaṁ diśō bhūrmahōdadhiḥ,

vāsudevasya vīryeṇa vidhṛtāni mahātmanaḥ.||14||

The sky, sun, moon, stars, space, directions, earth, and oceans are all held by Vasudeva's power.

sasurāsura-gandharvaṁ sayakṣōragarākṣasam,

jagad vaśe vartate idaṁ kṛṣṇasya sacarācaram.||15||

Everything in the universe, moving and unmoving, gods, demons, and others, are under Krishna's control.

indriyāṇi manō buddhiḥ sattvaṁ tejo balaṁ dhṛtiḥ,

vāsudevātmakāny āhuḥ kṣetraṁ kṣetrajña eva ca.||16||

The senses, mind, intellect, strength, and patience—all are said to be of Vasudeva's essence.

sarvāgamānām ācāraḥ prathamaṁ parikalpyate,

ācāra-prabhavo dharmo dharmasya prabhur acyutaḥ.||17||

All scriptures begin with right conduct; from conduct arises Dharma, and Lord Acyuta is its source.

ṛṣayaḥ pitarō devā mahābhūtāni dhātavaḥ,

jaṅgamājaṅgamaṁ cedaṁ jagan nārāyaṇodbhavam.||18||

Sages, ancestors, gods, elements, metals, living and non-living—everything originates from Narayana.

yōgō jñānaṁ tathā sāṅkhyaṁ vidyāḥ śilpādi karma ca,

vedāḥ śāstrāṇi vijñānam etat sarvaṁ janārdanāt.||19||

Yoga, knowledge, science, art, skills, Vedas, scriptures—all come from Janardana.

ekō viṣṇur mahadbhūtaṁ pṛthak bhūtāny anekaśaḥ,

trīn-lōkān vyāpya bhūtātmā bhuṅkte viśva-bhug avyayaḥ.||20||

Vishnu, the great being, though one, appears as many and pervades the three worlds as the eternal soul.

imaṁ stavaṁ bhagavato viṣṇor vyāsena kīrtitam,

paṭhet ya icchet puruṣaḥ śreyaḥ prāptuṁ sukhāni ca.||21||

Anyone who wishes for well-being and happiness should recite this hymn of Vishnu composed by Vyasa.

viśveśvaram ajaṁ devaṁ jagataḥ prabhavāpyayam,

bhajanti ye puṣkarākṣaṁ na te yānti parābhavam.||22||

Those who worship the lotus-eyed, unborn Lord of the universe never face defeat.

arjuna uvāca:

padmapatra-viśālākṣa padmanābha surottama,

bhaktānām anuraktānāṁ trātā bhava janārdana.||23||

Arjuna said: O lotus-eyed, lotus-naveled, best of gods—be the savior of your devoted followers, O Janardana.

śrī bhagavān uvāca:

yo māṁ nāma-sahasreṇa stotum icchati pāṇḍava,

soham ekena ślokena stuta eva na saṁśayaḥ.||24||

Lord Krishna said: O Arjuna, one who wishes to praise me with a thousand names may do so with just one stanza—I am pleased nonetheless.

vyāsa uvāca:

vāsanād vāsudevasya vāsitaṁ jagat trayam,

sarva-bhūta-nivāsosi vāsudeva namo'stu te.//25//

Vyasa said: Because of Vasudeva's presence, the three worlds exist. He resides in all beings. I bow to you, Vasudeva.

pārvaty uvāca:

kenopāyena laghunā viṣṇor nāma-sahasrakam,

paṭhyate bhakti-yuktaiḥ me śrotum icchāmy ahaṁ prabho.//26//

Parvati said: O Lord, by what simple means can devoted people recite the thousand names of Vishnu? I wish to know.

CHAPTER 4. - PRONUNCIATION GUIDE

Why Pronunciation Matters

When chanting the Sri Vishnu Sahasranama, each name of the Lord is more than a word—it is a vibrational key. These sacred names, when pronounced correctly, produce energetic effects that align our inner being with cosmic rhythms. Sanskrit is a vibrational language, where even a small change in sound can alter the intended energy. This is why pronunciation, especially while using English transliteration, is so important.

Even if Sanskrit is not your mother tongue, sincere effort and mindful articulation can still awaken its spiritual potency. This guide will help you chant with clarity, confidence, and devotion—whether silently in your heart or aloud with your breath.

Understanding Sanskrit Sounds Through English Letters

Sanskrit contains specific sounds that do not have exact equivalents in English. Hence, transliteration serves as a bridge—but not a perfect one. Let's begin by mapping common Sanskrit sounds too familiar English approximations.

Sanskrit	Sound	Pronunciation Tips
a	uh	Like 'a' in "sofa", short and soft
ā	aa	Like 'a' in "father", long and open
i	ih	Like 'i' in "bit", short and crisp
ī	ee	Like 'ee' in "see", long and smooth
u	uh	Like 'u' in "put", short and round
ū	oo	Like 'oo' in "boot", long and full
ṛ	ri	A blend of 'ri' in "ripple" and the tongue rolled slightly
e	ay	Like 'ay' in "say", always long
ai	eye	Like 'i' in "ice"
o	oh	Like 'o' in "go", not 'aw'
au	ow	Like 'ow' in "cow"

Practice Tip: Spend time on long vs. short vowels. Chanting "rama" (short 'a') vs "rāma" (long 'ā') changes the spiritual identity invoked.

Consonants

Sanskrit consonants are precise. Many are pronounced with specific tongue placements.

Letter	Example	Sound Tip
k	kāla	Like 'k' in "kite"
kh	khaga	'k' with a breathy burst—*aspirated k*
g	gati	Like 'g' in "go"
gh	ghana	'g' with aspiration
ṅ	aṅga	Like 'ng' in "song"
c	candra	Like 'ch' in "churn" (not 's' or 'k')
ch	chāyā	Stronger 'ch' with breath
j	jaya	Like 'j' in "joy"
jh	jñāna	Aspirated 'j'—rare in English
ñ	jñāna	'ny' as in "canyon"
ṭ	ṭīkṣṇa	Retroflex 't'—tongue curled back
ṭh	ṭhākur	Retroflex with aspiration
ḍ	ḍara	Retroflex 'd'

Letter	Example	Sound Tip
ḍh	ḍhana	Retroflex with breath
ṇ	śeṇa	Retroflex 'n'
t	tanu	Dental 't'—tongue on upper teeth
th	thāla	Dental 't' with breath
d	deva	Dental 'd'—tongue on teeth
dh	dharma	Aspirated 'd'
n	nāma	Like 'n' in "name"
p	puṣpa	Like 'p' in "pot"
ph	phala	Aspirated 'p', *not* 'f'
b	bhakti	Like 'b' in "boy"
bh	bhūmi	Aspirated 'b'
m	mantra	Like 'm' in "man"
y	yoga	Like 'y' in "yes"
r	rāma	Rolled or tapped tongue
l	lakṣmī	Like 'l' in "love"
v	veda	Between 'v' and 'w' in sound
ś	śiva	Soft 'sh' as in "shimmer"

Letter	Example	Sound Tip
ṣ	puruṣa	Harder 'sh', retroflex
s	sahasra	Like 's' in "sun"
h	hari	Like 'h' in "heart"

Practice Tip: Retroflex sounds (ṭ, ḍ, ṇ) are unique to Sanskrit. Curl your tongue back gently toward the palate to pronounce them.

Symbols in Transliteration

You'll encounter various diacritics (dots, macrons) in English transliteration of Sanskrit:

- **Macron (ā, ī, ū)**: Indicates a long vowel
- **Dot below (ṭ, ḍ, ṇ, ṣ)**: Retroflex consonant
- **Dot above (ṅ, ñ)**: Nasalized sounds

These marks are critical. "Nara" (man) and "Nāra" (divine being) have vastly different meanings—and energies.

Common Patterns in Vishnu Sahasranama

Let's examine recurring names and phrases to learn pronunciation by example.

1. Common Prefixes and Roots

- **Viṣṇu** – Pronounced *Vish-nu*, with a soft "ṣ"
- **Bhūta** – *Bhoo-ta*, where "ū" is long and "t" is dental

- **Puruṣa** – *Pu-roo-sha*, retroflex "ṣ"
- **Śrī** – *Shree*, soft "ś" and long "ī"
- **Jñāna** – *Gya-na* or *Gnya-na*, a nasal-palatal combo
- **Satya** – *Sut-ya* or *Sut-yah*, not "Sāt-yah"

Note: Avoid Anglicizing Sanskrit into "Vish-noo" or "Sri" as "sree." Preserve vowel length.

2. Full Name Practice

Try chanting and breaking names into syllables:

- **Viśvaṁ viṣṇur vaṣaṭkāro bhūta-bhavya-bhavat-prabhuḥ**
    - *Vish-vam Vish-nur Va-shat-ka-ro Bhoo-ta Bhav-ya Bha-vat Pra-bhooh*
- **Bhūta-kṛd bhūta-bhṛd bhāvo bhūtātmā bhūta-bhāvanaḥ**
    - *Bhoo-ta-krit Bhoo-ta-bhrid Bha-vo Bhoo-taat-maa Bhoo-ta-bhaa-va-naḥ*

Chant slowly, pause where commas fall, and respect long vowels. You'll begin to feel the rhythm naturally.

Chanting Tips for Beginners

1. Start Slow

Chant 5–10 names daily with correct pronunciation rather than rushing through all 1000 incorrectly. Quality over quantity.

2. Record Yourself

Use a recording app to play back and self-correct your enunciation.

3. Listen to Masters

Find audio renditions by Sanskrit scholars (e.g. MS Subbulakshmi, Swami Brahmananda). Mimic their tone and pacing.

4. Practice with Transliteration

Read from a printed or digital copy with transliteration. Sound each syllable with care.

Common Pronunciation Errors to Avoid

Incorrect	Correct	Explanation
Vishnu	Viṣṇu	Use "ṣ" for retroflex 'sh'
Rama	Rāma	Long 'ā' is essential
Krishna	Kṛṣṇa	Retroflex 'ṣ', rolled 'ṛ'
Shree	Śrī	Use soft 'ś' and long 'ī'
Prabhu	Prabhuḥ	Don't drop final 'ḥ'—a soft breathy 'h'
Aum	Om	Pronounced as *A-U-M*, not a flat 'Ohm'

Note: Even advanced speakers slip into anglicized habits—stay mindful.

Chanting as Meditation

Pronunciation becomes deeper when paired with **intention**. Don't treat this guide as a set of rules; treat it as **a map to spiritual clarity**. Every name is a mantric code, each syllable a spark of cosmic light.

Sample Meditation Exercise

- Sit comfortably. Breathe deeply.
- Chant: **"Om Namo Bhagavate Vāsudevāya"**

- *Om Na-mo Bha-ga-va-te Vaa-su-de-va-ya*

- Repeat 9 times, focusing on each syllable.
- Feel the vibration flow through your spine and chest.

Pronunciation & Energy: A Vibrational Insight

Modern studies on sound healing align with what ancient Rishis knew: sound shapes consciousness. Words like Viṣṇu, Kṛṣṇa, Śānti, and Mokṣa are not just poetic—they emit frequencies that alter brainwaves, heart rate, and energy fields.

Sanskrit = Sonic Yoga

Chanting correctly becomes a form of vocal yoga—a harmonization of tongue, breath, and awareness.

Final Words: Faith Over Perfection

If you're afraid of getting it wrong—don't be.

Sanskrit is forgiving when paired with bhakti (devotion). Lord Vishnu does not demand perfection; He responds to **intent and sincerity**. Still, making an effort to pronounce His names correctly is an act of love and reverence.

Appendix: Quick Recap of Pronunciation Keys

- Long vowels (ā, ī, ū) matter deeply—length = energy
- Retroflex consonants (ṭ, ḍ, ṇ, ṣ) require tongue curling
- 'ḥ' at the end (visarga) = gentle, breathy 'h' sound
- Chant slowly, clearly, and from the diaphragm
- Follow natural breaks; don't rush through compound words

CHAPTER 5. - HISTORICAL SIGNIFICANCE

The *Sri Vishnu Sahasranama*—a sacred compilation of a thousand names

of Lord Vishnu—is not merely a hymn; it is a window into the spiritual, historical, and cultural heritage of ancient India. It has been chanted, revered, and preserved for thousands of years, continuously echoing through the voices of saints, kings, and householders alike.

Understanding its historical significance allows us to appreciate not only its devotional beauty but also its role as a bridge between Vedic wisdom, political leadership, classical education, and regional identity. This chapter explores the origins, preservation, dissemination, and influence of this hymn across time.

1. Origins in the Mahabharata

The Vishnu Sahasranama is sourced from **Book 13 (Anushasana Parva)** of the *Mahabharata*, one of the two great Sanskrit epics of India. It emerges during a deeply poignant moment: the noble warrior Bhishma lies wounded on the bed of arrows on the battlefield of Kurukshetra, awaiting death.

In the presence of Lord Krishna, Bhishma imparts his final teachings to the eldest Pandava, **Yudhishthira**—teachings meant to anchor a king's mind and a nation's dharma during a period of collapse and moral confusion. Among these is the chanting of the thousand names of Vishnu, offered as a **universal solution to suffering and confusion**.

This setting is deeply symbolic:

- Bhishma symbolizes wisdom accumulated through lifetimes.
- Yudhishthira represents the seeker caught in conflict.
- Krishna embodies the divine presence guiding truth through chaos.

Why This Moment Matters

The fact that *Sri Vishnu Sahasranama* is delivered at the end of a catastrophic war, and not during a temple ritual or quiet forest, shows its intent: this chant is for the householders, rulers, and every soul struggling with life—not just for sages in isolation.

2. Composition and Structure

The Vishnu Sahasranama is composed in **Anushtup meter**, a common meter used in classical Sanskrit literature, including the Bhagavad Gita. The names are organized not randomly but thematically and rhythmically, encompassing divine attributes such as:

- Omniscience (*Sarvajñaḥ*)
- Compassion (*Kṛpāluḥ*)
- Cosmic Support (*Dhātā, Viśvadhṛg*)
- Warrior Energy (*Mahāvīryaḥ, Jetā*)
- Inner Witness (*Sākṣī*)

These 1000 names are not arbitrary; they are the **compressed scriptural DNA** of the Vishnu Purana, Upanishadic truths, and Itihasa traditions.

3. Preservation Through Oral Tradition

India's knowledge systems were primarily preserved **orally for millennia**, and the Vishnu Sahasranama benefited from this tradition. The text was:

- Memorized by families and students from childhood
- Chanted in daily and ceremonial worship
- Sung in temples during *puja*, *archana*, and *yajna*
- Transmitted across regions through **parampara** (lineages)

This ensured not only accurate pronunciation but also cultural transmission. The chant became **part of the living heritage**, not merely a textual artifact.

Role of Gurukulas and Temples

From Kerala's Vedic pathashalas to Tamil Nadu's Divya Desham temples, from Odia Vaishnava centers to Maharashtra's Bhakti sampradayas, Vishnu Sahasranama has remained a **central text in teaching devotion, discipline, and Sanskrit pronunciation.**

4. The Bhakti Movement and Vernacular Spread

Between the 7th and 15th centuries CE, India witnessed the **Bhakti Movement**, which democratized devotion. Saints like:

- **Alwars** in Tamil Nadu,
- **Namdev and Tukaram** in Maharashtra,
- **Surdas and Tulsidas** in North India,
- **Chaitanya Mahaprabhu** in Bengal

...often referred to the **names of the Divine** as their chosen path to salvation. Many used the *Vishnu Sahasranama* or similar name-lists (*nama-sankirtana*) as part of their practice.

In this era, the chant moved from Sanskrit circles into the hands and homes of ordinary people—*housewives, farmers, traders, and kings*—through **local translations, melodies, and explanations.**

5. Philosophical Interpretations Across Schools

The Vishnu Sahasranama's power lies not only in its poetry but in its **universality across Vedantic schools**.

Adi Shankaracharya (8th century CE)

A champion of **Advaita Vedanta**, Shankara wrote an influential **commentary** (bhashya) on the Sahasranama, interpreting the names as referring to **Nirguna Brahman**—the formless, infinite consciousness.

His bhashya elevated the Sahasranama beyond ritual into **Jnana Yoga** (path of knowledge), without denying its devotional appeal.

Ramanujacharya (11th century CE)

Ramanuja, proponent of **Vishishtadvaita**, saw the names as reflecting the **Saguna Brahman**—a personal, loving deity with divine qualities. He encouraged **daily chanting** as a means of surrender (*prapatti*) and liberation.

Madhvacharya (13th century CE)

As the founder of **Dvaita philosophy**, Madhva upheld Lord Vishnu as a distinct and supreme reality. His followers used the Sahasranama as **proof of divine hierarchy**, with Vishnu at the apex.

6. Royal Patronage and Political Legacy

Historically, kings across India used the Vishnu Sahasranama as a **guide for righteous rule** and personal discipline. Inscriptions, temple endowments, and royal oaths often invoked names like:

- *Dharma-yūpaḥ* (pillar of justice)
- *Rāmaḥ* (ideal ruler)
- *Viśvabāhuḥ* (supporter of the world)

Examples of Royal Use

- **Gupta Empire (4th–6th century CE):** Embraced Vaishnavism and sponsored temple chantings.
- **Chola and Vijayanagar Kings (9th–16th centuries):** Installed Sahasranama panels in temple halls.

- **Mughal & Maratha Periods:** Despite varied rule, the Sahasranama survived due to strong **community practice**.

7. Modern Revival and Global Reach

In the last 100 years, the Vishnu Sahasranama has been **revived in new formats**:

Print and Media

- Popularized through books, vinyl records, cassettes, and digital media
- English transliterations have made it globally accessible
- Radio and TV shows like "Ramayan" and "Mahabharat" popularized its verses

Institutions and Movements

- **ISKCON**, **Chinmaya Mission**, and **Ramakrishna Math** promote it in global satsangs.
- It is chanted in daily morning prayers in many South Indian households and temples abroad—from Canada to Malaysia.

8. Influence on Language, Art, and Culture

Language

The names of Lord Vishnu, especially from the Sahasranama, became **common given names**:

- *Madhava, Keshava, Govinda, Narayan*

They also became part of *greetings* and *blessings*, like:

- **"Om Namo Narayanaya"**

- **“Govinda Govinda”** during crises or celebrations

Art and Sculpture

Temples often depict Sahasranama names in:

- Carvings on stone pillars
- Altar backdrops (e.g., Tirupati, Srirangam)
- Tanjore and Pattachitra paintings

9. Cross-Sectarian Appeal

Although it is technically a Vaishnava chant, the Vishnu Sahasranama is embraced by:

- **Shaivites**: As an acknowledgment of Vishnu’s role in the cosmic trinity
- **Smarta followers**: As one of the pancha-devata paths
- **Buddhists and Jains**: For its meditative phonetics and ethical beauty

Its **neutral tone**, lack of sectarian bias, and universal spiritual appeal have made it a **shared cultural treasure**.

10. Historical Resilience: Surviving Time and Turmoil

The most incredible historical significance of the Vishnu Sahasranama is its **resilience**. Despite:

- Foreign invasions
- Colonial interruptions
- Cultural fragmentation

...it has continued **uninterrupted in oral, written, and living form**. It is one of the few chants known, memorized, and recited across **age groups, castes, regions, and languages**.

CHAPTER 6. - SCIENTIFIC BENEFITS OF CHANTING

What if thousands of years of spiritual tradition had hidden within it a subtle science—one that could enhance mental clarity, emotional resilience, physical well-being, and even spiritual consciousness? For centuries, saints and seekers have said that **chanting the names of the Divine brings peace, healing, and transformation**. Today, science is beginning to catch up.

The *Sri Vishnu Sahasranama* is not just a devotional recitation—it is a **vibrational technology**. Its 1000 names are crafted in Sanskrit, a language designed not just for meaning but for **resonance**. When you chant these names, you're not only invoking divinity—you are activating your **brain, breath, and biology**.

This chapter will explore the **scientific benefits of chanting**, with a focus on the Vishnu Sahasranama, and show why what the ancients practiced intuitively is now validated through neuroscience, sound therapy, epigenetics, and psychology.

1. The Neuroscience of Mantra Chanting

Brain Waves and Mental State

Modern neuroscience has discovered that chanting mantras has a powerful impact on brainwaves. In particular, it activates:

- **Alpha Waves** (8–12 Hz): Associated with calm, wakeful relaxation
- **Theta Waves** (4–7 Hz): Linked to meditation, memory, and deep creativity

Scientific Insight:
A study conducted at the University of West Virginia found that mantra meditation significantly increases alpha activity and reduces beta wave dominance (associated with anxiety and active thinking). This shift in brainwave frequency mimics the relaxed state seen in experienced meditators and even in advanced yogic samadhis.

When you chant *Viṣṇur vaṣaṭkāraḥ*, you are not just pronouncing syllables—you are creating a neural environment conducive to **mental clarity and emotional balance**.

2. Vagal Toning and the Nervous System

Your **vagus nerve** is the largest cranial nerve, extending from the brainstem to the abdomen. It regulates the **parasympathetic nervous system**—the "rest and digest" mode that promotes calmness, digestion, and immune repair.

Chanting stimulates the vagus nerve

- Sounds like "Om" and "Namah" create vibrations in the chest and throat, directly activating this nerve.
- This stimulation **lowers heart rate**, **reduces cortisol (stress hormone)**, and **increases serotonin** (the happiness molecule).

Scientific Insight:
In 2010, a study in the *International Journal of Yoga* confirmed that chanting "Om" activates brain regions related to relaxation, including the limbic system, and improves vagal tone—associated with **greater emotional resilience and heart health**.

3. Mantras and Heart-Brain Coherence

HeartMath Institute, a pioneer in neurocardiology, has shown that chanting and rhythmic breathing create **heart-brain coherence**, a state where your heart rate variability (HRV) and brain rhythms synchronize. This state:

- Reduces anxiety
- Enhances decision-making
- Improves immunity
- Increases intuitive awareness

Chanting *Viṣṇave Prabhaviṣṇave* in a slow, rhythmic pace regulates your breath naturally. Over time, it creates a **feedback loop of emotional stability, resilience, and clarity**.

4. Sound Frequencies and Cellular Health

The human body is largely made of water—about 60% in adults. Sound travels faster through water than air, and each chant **sends vibrations into your tissues**, organs, and even cells.

Sanskrit Mantras and Healing Frequencies

- The Sanskrit syllables in Vishnu Sahasranama are tuned to specific **frequencies** and **resonant patterns**.
- These frequencies have been shown to influence **cellular activity**, including:
    - DNA repair
    - Blood pressure regulation
    - Pain perception

Scientific Insight:
A 2016 study published in *Journal of Traditional and Complementary Medicine* demonstrated that mantras like "Om" produce vibrations that help regulate nitric oxide in cells—supporting **blood flow, immunity, and detoxification**.

5. Memory and Cognitive Enhancement

Chanting Vishnu Sahasranama daily involves learning and recalling 1000 unique names—each with different meanings and pronunciations. This activity strengthens:

- **Auditory memory**
- **Pattern recognition**
- **Verbal retention**
- **Attention span**

Cognitive Benefits of Repetition

Scientific research has consistently shown that **repetition with rhythm**—as in mantra chanting—enhances **neuroplasticity**, the brain's ability to form and strengthen new neural connections. This helps in:

- Delaying cognitive decline
- Improving focus and attention
- Enhancing learning capacity in children and elders alike

6. Emotional Regulation and Mental Health

Mantras as Cognitive Reframing Tools

Every name in Vishnu Sahasranama is a positive affirmation:

- *Bhaktavatsalaḥ* – "The one who loves devotees deeply"
- *Kṣemakṛt* – "The giver of well-being"
- *Anantaḥ* – "The limitless one"

Chanting these repeatedly rewires the subconscious mind with **faith, security, and trust**. This acts as **cognitive reframing**, replacing fear-based thought patterns with ones rooted in surrender and peace.

Stress and Anxiety Relief

- Studies show that chanting mantras for 15 minutes a day reduces **amygdala activity** (the brain's fear center).
- It increases **GABA**, the neurotransmitter responsible for calming the nervous system.

A 2017 paper in *Frontiers in Human Neuroscience* concluded that mantric repetition significantly **lowers depression and anxiety scores**, even in clinical populations.

7. Respiratory Benefits and Pranic Control

Chanting naturally slows and deepens the breath, creating a bridge to the **autonomic nervous system**. Most mantras, including *Om Namo Narayanaya*, are chanted in a **1:1 or 2:1 breathing ratio**, which improves:

- **Lung capacity**
- **Oxygen absorption**
- **Breath awareness (pranayama)**

This creates a state of **pranic coherence**, optimizing energy flow in the body and calming the mind. It's no surprise that many practitioners report feeling **energized yet grounded** after a chanting session.

8. Group Chanting and Social Resonance

Science shows that **group chanting** leads to social synchronization. When people chant together:

- Their heartbeats and breathing rhythms begin to align.
- Oxytocin (bonding hormone) is released.
- Feelings of separation and loneliness dissolve.

This is why temples, satsangs, and bhajan gatherings generate a feeling of **oneness and elevation**—what the ancients called *satsangha* and what modern science calls **entrainment**.

9. Mantras and Epigenetics

Emerging research in **epigenetics**—the study of how environment and behavior affect gene expression—suggests that **consistent mantra chanting can influence gene activity**.

- Regular chanting reduces expression of genes related to **inflammation, cortisol production**, and **oxidative stress**.
- It may activate genes responsible for **longevity, cellular repair, and neural regeneration**.

This aligns with what Ayurveda and yogic sciences have long claimed: **your internal vibration shapes your biology**.

10. Placebo or Beyond? The Power of Belief and Intention

Skeptics often attribute mantra benefits to the **placebo effect**—but this is a powerful mechanism in itself.

- When you **believe** in a sacred chant's power, your brain produces real biochemical changes.
- Combined with **intention** (called *bhāva* in Sanskrit), this creates a psycho-spiritual field conducive to **healing, transformation, and insight**.

Thus, whether you approach the Vishnu Sahasranama as sacred or simply as sound medicine, its effects are **undeniable and measurable**.

Case Study: Vishnu Sahasranama and Holistic Health

Dr. Raghunathan, a neurologist in Bengaluru, introduced Vishnu Sahasranama chanting to a group of patients with stress-related insomnia. Over 8 weeks:

- 76% reported improved sleep
- 63% experienced reduced anxiety
- 42% showed lower blood pressure

He notes:

"It is as if the nervous system listens to the chant more deeply than the mind does. The patients found themselves soothed even when they didn't understand every name. Something primal responded."

Spiritual Science: Going Beyond the Brain

While modern science focuses on **neural mechanisms**, the Rishis emphasized **subtle energies**. According to yogic science:

- Every mantra activates **chakras** (energy centers)
- Vishnu Sahasranama particularly resonates with:

- **Anahata (Heart)** – fostering devotion and balance
- **Ajna (Third Eye)** – enhancing insight and discrimination
- **Sahasrara (Crown)** – opening higher consciousness

Thus, the Sahasranama becomes both **sound therapy and soul therapy**.

CHAPTER 7. - STORIES & ANECDOTES

Stories are not just entertainment—they are mirrors. In every tale of faith and transformation lies a reflection of what is possible for us. The *Sri Vishnu Sahasranama* is more than a list of divine names; it is a lifeline. Across centuries, countless lives have been touched, transformed, and even saved by the simple act of chanting these sacred syllables.

This chapter gathers stories from scripture, folklore, saints, and everyday people—each bearing witness to the **power of divine remembrance**. Some are miraculous, some humble, but all echo a single truth: **when you call out His thousand names, He listens.**

1. Bhishma on the Bed of Arrows

Let us begin with the origin itself. *Bhishma Pitamah*, mortally wounded on the battlefield of Kurukshetra, chose to delay his death until the auspicious time of *Uttarayana*. While he lay in unimaginable pain on a bed of arrows, he shared with Yudhishthira his final wisdom—including the Vishnu Sahasranama.

Why is this powerful?

Because Bhishma was not a recluse or a mystic—he was a warrior, a statesman, a leader. And when he had to offer his most potent advice to the future king, he chose **a hymn. A chant. A stream of names.**

He said to Yudhishthira:

"He who chants these names with devotion, even once, will be freed from fear, sin, and suffering. There is no greater means than this."

That is the weight of this chant. It was given not in a classroom, but in a battlefield. Not in theory, but through experience.

2. The King Who Found Peace

Centuries ago, in the ancient kingdom of Vidarbha, a just but anxious king named Haridas was tormented by constant worry. Despite wealth, family, and fame, he couldn't sleep. Seeking relief, he approached a wandering sadhu.

The sadhu gave him no herbs, no incantations—only a tattered palm leaf containing the **Vishnu Sahasranama**.

"Read just a few names each night," the sadhu said, "and you will sleep in the lap of God."

The king obeyed. That night, he read the first ten names aloud. He slept deeply for the first time in years.

Eventually, the king began chanting the entire Sahasranama before bed. His anxiety faded, his rule flourished, and his people called him **"Raja Vishnupriya"**—the king beloved of Vishnu.

3. The Boy Who Remembered

In a small Tamil village, a ten-year-old boy named Kannan was once caught in a storm on his way home from school. Frightened and alone, he recalled the only prayer his grandmother taught him: the opening verse of the Vishnu Sahasranama.

Huddled under a banyan tree, he chanted:

Viśvaṁ viṣṇur vaṣaṭkāraḥ bhūta-bhavya-bhavat-prabhuḥ...

The rain calmed. A passerby spotted him and offered shelter. When asked what gave him courage, the boy simply said, "**Narayana was with me**. I called Him, and He came."

That boy grew up to be a spiritual teacher. His first and favorite lesson? "**When afraid, chant the names of Vishnu. Fear will disappear.**"

4. Ramanuja's Childhood Miracle

The revered Vaishnava acharya **Ramanujacharya** was once gravely ill as a child. His mother, believing in the healing power of devotion, sat by his bedside chanting the Vishnu Sahasranama.

As she reached the verse **"Anādinidhanō viṣṇuṁ sarvalokamaheśvaram,"** Ramanuja, unconscious until then, stirred and slowly opened his eyes.

He later wrote that he had seen a golden form standing beside him, whose eyes were like lotuses and who spoke gently:

"My name will protect you. Always keep it in your heart."

Ramanuja would go on to promote the Sahasranama as the easiest path to liberation in the Kali Yuga.

5. The Saint Who Forgot Himself

Swami Haridas, a wandering saint in North India, once took a vow of silence. For twelve years, he did not speak to anyone. He spent his days in the forests near Vrindavan, chanting the Vishnu Sahasranama from dawn to dusk.

One day, a wild tiger approached him. But the Swami did not react. He was in such deep immersion in chanting that he **had no fear, no awareness of the external world**.

Witnesses later said the tiger sat in front of him for a few moments, then quietly turned away.

When asked later if he had seen the tiger, Swami Haridas smiled and said,

"I only saw Vishnu... a thousand forms, a thousand lights. Perhaps the tiger saw Him too."

6. The Modern-Day Executive

Arvind, a stressed software executive in Bengaluru, was burning out. Deadlines, insomnia, family tensions—he had tried everything from yoga to therapy. Then, a colleague casually mentioned the Vishnu Sahasranama.

Skeptical but desperate, Arvind downloaded a recording and played it during his morning commute. Within weeks:

- He was sleeping better.
- His blood pressure dropped.
- He smiled more.

He didn't understand Sanskrit. He didn't even identify as "religious." Yet, he says:

"There's a silence behind the names. Something ancient. Something intelligent. It saved me."

Today, Arvind teaches the chant to his children—not as a ritual, but as a **resilience practice**.

7. The Old Widow's Gift

In a small village in Andhra Pradesh lived an old widow named Janaki Amma. She had no formal education, no family left, and very little income. Yet every evening, her voice would fill the neighbourhood as she chanted the Vishnu Sahasranama from memory.

When asked how she remembered so much, she said,

"My husband taught me one name a day for 1000 days. I haven't forgotten a single one."

One year, during a local drought, villagers gathered to pray for rain. Janaki Amma led the prayer—not with rituals, but by chanting all 1000 names aloud.

The next morning, it rained for the first time in months.

8. The Prisoner's Redemption

In the early 1990s, a convict in Tihar Jail was sentenced to life for murder. Isolated and bitter, he refused to speak or eat. A volunteer from a local temple gave him a pocket-sized book of Vishnu Sahasranama and simply said, "You can't escape this place. But you can escape yourself."

The man ignored it for weeks. One sleepless night, he opened the book and began reading aloud.

That was the beginning.

In 3 years:

- He became a model prisoner.
- He taught Sanskrit chants to other inmates.
- He said he felt **freer inside prison than ever outside.**

When released on parole, his first stop was a Vishnu temple. His only prayer:

"Thank You for letting me chant Your names even in darkness."

9. The Mother's Blessing

In Kerala, a mother once taught her child the Sahasranama not from a book but through lullabies. Every night, she would softly sing 10–20 names to lull the child to sleep.

Years later, the child—now a grown man—recalled that even during the hardest moments in life, when grief or anxiety overtook him, those names would suddenly surface:

"Anantaḥ, Hṛṣīkeśaḥ, Keśavaḥ..."

He didn't remember calculus or history from school. But he remembered the names.
Because they were sung with love. And love has memory.

10. The Lost-and-Found Child

A five-year-old girl in Mumbai once got separated from her parents during a crowded temple festival. Frightened, she sat under a tree and began softly chanting:

Om Namo Narayanaya... Om Namo Narayanaya...

A kind stranger heard her and asked her name. She said, "I don't know—but I'm chanting. Vishnu will help me."

The stranger brought her to the temple's lost child center. Minutes later, her parents arrived.

They asked her, "Weren't you scared?"
She replied:

"No. I was holding God's hand. I was chanting."

CHAPTER 8. - REGIONAL VARIATIONS & TRADITIONS

The *Sri Vishnu Sahasranama* is like a river that began in the high mountains of ancient scriptures and has flowed across regions, languages, and generations—touching every shore it reached in a different way.

Though the original Sanskrit version comes from the *Mahabharata*, the Vishnu Sahasranama has been adopted and loved by **millions of devotees** across India and the world. Every culture, language, and lineage has offered its own flavor—through melody, ritual, timing, and interpretation.

This chapter is an exploration of how the Vishnu Sahasranama is embraced regionally—proof that while the Divine Names remain the same, **the ways of worship reflect the heart of the devotee.**

1. South India: Devotion in Daily Life

Tamil Nadu: The Bhakti Bedrock

In Tamil Nadu, the Vishnu Sahasranama is deeply rooted in both **Vaishnava temples** and **household traditions**.

- Daily recitation is common in orthodox homes, especially on **Saturdays and Ekadashi**.

- Many people chant it in the **early morning or twilight (sandhya) hours**, often followed by other stotras like *Aditya Hridayam* or *Lalita Sahasranama*.

Divya Desams and Alwar Influence

- The 108 *Divya Desams*—sacred Vishnu temples sung by Alwars—often include Sahasranama chanting in temple rituals.
- Alwars like **Periyalvar and Nammazhwar** popularized the chanting of names (*namasankirtana*), inspiring the blending of scriptural chanting with **personal, emotional bhakti**.

Kerala: Melodic Discipline

In Kerala, Vishnu Sahasranama is recited with a **distinctive musical cadence**, often in a **slow, meditative rhythm**.

- It is commonly chanted after **Deeparadhana (evening lamp worship)**.
- Many temples, like **Guruvayur**, feature public chanting sessions (*samooha parayanam*).
- Elderly women in Kerala are known to have the entire text **memorized**, reciting it like a lullaby or a shield of prayer.

Andhra Pradesh & Telangana: Scriptural Integration

In Telugu-speaking regions:

- The Vishnu Sahasranama is often taught along with the **Bhagavad Gita**, as part of spiritual education for children.
- **Harikatha artists** integrate verses into musical storytelling.
- Temples like **Tirumala Tirupati** include daily or weekly Sahasranama chanting as part of their sevas (*ritual services*).

2. North India: Names as Remembrance

In northern states like Uttar Pradesh, Bihar, Rajasthan, and Madhya Pradesh, the Vishnu Sahasranama is less common in daily rituals, but remains highly respected.

Scriptural Chanting During Ceremonies

- The Sahasranama is often recited during **Gita Jayanti**, **Ekadashi**, or **Shraddha ceremonies** (ancestral rituals).
- Priests may include select verses in **Satyanarayan Puja**, invoking Vishnu's thousand-fold power.

Bhakti Movements and Simpler Forms

- Saints like **Tulsidas** and **Kabir** popularized **nama-smarana (name remembrance)** in simpler formats.
- While *Ram Nam* or *Hari Om* became more popular mantras in daily chanting, the Sahasranama remained a revered **scriptural cornerstone**.

3. Western India: Community and Tradition

Maharashtra: Sahasranama in Bhajans

The **Warkari movement** centered around Pandharpur and Vithoba worship brought bhakti into the hands of the people. Though the focus is often on **Vitthala-Rakhumai**, Vishnu Sahasranama is:

- Included in **bhajan gatherings** and **namasankirtanas**.
- Read aloud during **special festivals**, especially **Gita Jayanti**, **Vaikuntha Ekadashi**, and **Margashirsha** month.

Gujarat: Blending of Vaishnav and Shakta Traditions

In Vaishnav homes of Gujarat, especially among followers of **Pushtimarg (Vallabhacharya's tradition)**, the chant is used during:

- **Morning prayers (mangalacharan)**
- **Ekadashi fast-breaking rituals**
- Combined with **chanting of Ashtakshara (Om Namo Narayanaya)** or **Dwadashakshara mantra**

4. Eastern India: Grace in Simplicity

West Bengal and Odisha

Here, the chanting culture was deeply influenced by the **Chaitanya Mahaprabhu movement**, which prioritized **the Hare Krishna Mahamantra**. However:

- Many temples chant Vishnu Sahasranama on **Vaikuntha Ekadashi** and **Gita Jayanti**.
- Some schools include it in **evening prayers or Saraswati puja rituals**.

In Odisha, **Jagannath worship** connects strongly to Vishnu, and though local *bhajans* dominate, the Sahasranama is still respected as a **sacred recitation during yajnas and festivals.**

5. Himalayan Belt: Temples in the Clouds

In regions like Himachal Pradesh, Uttarakhand, and Jammu:

- Chanting is performed in **Vaishno Devi** and **Badrinath** temples during special *yagnas*.

- Pilgrims heading to Char Dham may carry a **pocket book of the Sahasranama**, chanting it along the trek.
- The chant is seen not only as **a prayer** but as **protection** in harsh conditions.

6. Global Traditions: Chanting Beyond Borders

Today, the Vishnu Sahasranama is recited not just across India, but globally.

In the Indian Diaspora

- **Temples in the US, UK, Canada, Singapore, and Australia** hold weekly Vishnu Sahasranama chanting groups.
- Families teach it to children using **Roman transliteration**, ensuring its transmission despite the loss of Sanskrit familiarity.

In Interfaith and Yoga Communities

- It is chanted in **kirtans**, **sound healing sessions**, and **yogic retreats**.
- Often seen as a **vibrational tool** rather than a religious chant.
- English-translated versions are used in **non-Indian spiritual groups**, emphasizing the universality of its meanings.

7. Gendered Traditions and Women's Devotion

Women have played a crucial role in preserving and passing down the Vishnu Sahasranama:

- **Grandmothers in Tamil Nadu** teach it as part of a girl's coming-of-age ritual.
- In Kerala, women chant it during **Vrata (fasting) days** like Ekadashi and Fridays.

- In Maharashtra, **Sahasranama groups run by women** gather every Saturday to chant and discuss meaning.

This chant has never been reserved for scholars alone. It lives **in the memory and voice of women**, often becoming the **first spiritual text learned by heart**.

8. Musical Variations

Each region brings its own **melody and rhythm** to the Sahasranama:

Region	**Style**	**Notes**
Tamil Nadu	*Chandas-based recitation*	Rhythmic and metered
Kerala	*Bhajan-style tune*	Melodic, slow-paced
Andhra	*Clear articulation*	Often performed with commentary (pravachan)
Gujarat	*Kirtan-friendly rhythm*	Lively and communal
US/UK Temples	*Call-and-response*	Inclusive for non-Sanskrit speakers

This musical diversity proves a deeper truth: **there's no single "right" way to chant**—only sincere intention.

9. Sacred Days and Ritual Uses

Across India and the diaspora, specific days are considered **highly auspicious for chanting Vishnu Sahasranama**:

- **Ekadashi (11th lunar day)** – especially **Vaikuntha Ekadashi**
- **Gita Jayanti** – the day Lord Krishna revealed the Gita
- **Saturdays** – associated with seeking protection from fears
- **Shravan month (July–August)** – ideal for spiritual practices
- **Karthika month (November)** – considered sacred for Vishnu

In **household rituals**, the chant is used during:

- **Birth ceremonies**
- **Upanayanam (sacred thread)** rituals
- **Marriage functions**
- **Shraddha (ancestral homage)**

CHAPTER 9. - MEDITATION & VISUALIZATION TECHNIQUES

The *Sri Vishnu Sahasranama* is not just a chant to be recited—it is a **journey inward**, a form of **sound meditation** that leads the mind to silence and the heart to presence. Beyond repetition lies realization. Beyond the thousand names lies the **formless Vishnu**, waiting to reveal Himself in your inner space.

This chapter explores how to deepen your experience of the Sahasranama through **meditation and visualization techniques**. Whether you're a beginner seeking calm or a seasoned practitioner yearning for communion, these methods invite you to make each name a doorway to **stillness, grace, and inner transformation**.

1. Mantra Meditation: Chanting as Mindful Presence

Chanting the Vishnu Sahasranama can itself be a form of **japa meditation** when done with focused awareness.

How to Practice:

1. Sit comfortably, spine straight, eyes closed or lowered.
2. Take 3 deep breaths to center yourself.
3. Begin chanting the names slowly, either aloud or mentally.
4. With each name, try to **listen fully**, without rushing.
5. Notice when the mind wanders and gently return to the next name.
6. After finishing, sit in silence for a few minutes.

What This Cultivates:

- **Dharana** (concentration)
- **Dhyana** (meditative absorption)
- An effortless state of **flow and devotion**

Even chanting just 20–30 names with complete awareness can shift your mental state from agitation to **spiritual attunement**.

2. Name Meditation: One Name, One Day

This technique involves selecting **one name of Vishnu each day** and meditating on its meaning, form, and feeling.

Steps:

- Choose a name (e.g., *Vāsudeva, Ananta, Govinda*)
- Repeat it **108 times** mentally or with a japa mala
- Reflect on:
    - What does this name mean?
    - What image or emotion does it evoke?
    - Where do I see this quality in my life?
- Sit in silent contemplation for 5–10 minutes afterward

Benefits:

- Deepens **emotional connection** with the Divine
- Builds familiarity with the thousand names one-by-one
- Turns each name into a **personal revelation**

You may journal your reflections or sketch images associated with the name. Over time, your relationship with Vishnu becomes **intimate and living.**

3. Visualization: Seeing the Lord Within

Visualization is a powerful method in traditional Indian meditation systems, known as **dhyana yoga**. In this approach, you **mentally construct an image** of Vishnu, allowing the mind to stabilize in beauty, devotion, and transcendence.

Simple Vishnu Visualization:

1. Sit in stillness.
2. As you chant a verse (e.g., *Viśvam Viṣṇur Vaṣaṭkāraḥ...*), visualize:
    - A radiant blue form sitting on a **lotus throne**
    - Four arms holding **Shankha (conch), Chakra (discus), Gada (mace), and Padma (lotus)**
    - Eyes filled with compassion
    - Surrounded by divine light or floating on **Ananta-Shesha**
3. Feel His presence entering your heart. Let this image grow until it fills your inner space.

You are not imagining the form—you are **remembering** it. It already exists within you.

Why This Works:

- Anchors the **wandering mind**
- Awakens the **heart's bhakti (devotion)**
- Deepens your connection to **Sākāra (form-based)** meditation

4. Breath-Linked Chanting: Nama + Pranayama

Marrying the breath with chanting creates a **symphony of rhythm and stillness**. This method is ideal for those with a pranayama or yoga background.

Breath Practice:

- Inhale: mentally chant "Om Namo"
- Exhale: chant "Bhagavate Vāsudevāya" or another name
- Alternatively, chant one full name per complete breath cycle

This style naturally slows down the chant, allowing the **prana (vital energy)** to become infused with **nama (divine name)**.

It brings the chant **from the throat to the heart to the breath**—a full-body meditative experience.

5. Chakra Meditation with the Names

The Vishnu Sahasranama can also be used in **chakra-based meditation**, aligning divine qualities with energy centers in the body.

Example Technique:

Choose a name and locate its resonance in the body.

Chakra	Sample Names	Feeling/Meaning
Root (Muladhara)	*Adhokṣaja, Puruṣa*	Groundedness, cosmic presence
Sacral (Svadhisthana)	*Kāma-nāśana, Bhūta-kṛt*	Purification, vitality
Solar Plexus (Manipura)	*Mahā-veerya, Jetā*	Strength, leadership
Heart (Anahata)	*Bhaktavatsala, Kṛṣṇa*	Love, grace
Throat (Vishuddha)	*Nārāyaṇa, Viṣṇu*	Sound, truth, expression
Third Eye (Ajna)	*Yogī, Sākṣī*	Insight, perception
Crown (Sahasrara)	*Ananta, Govinda, Sarveśvara*	Unity, divine awareness

As you chant or think the name, visualize energy glowing in that center.

This technique is **powerful for both healing and awakening**.

6. Silent Internal Recitation: The Inward Mantra

Beyond audible chanting lies **mānasa japa**—mental repetition of the names, often described as the **most refined form of devotion**.

How to practice:

- Sit in stillness.
- Mentally repeat each name silently.
- Imagine it as a light or mantra dropping gently into the heart.

- Allow no sound, no movement—only inner awareness of each syllable.

This method brings deep calm and inner stillness. In time, the mantra may begin to **repeat itself**—a sign of deep absorption (*ajapa japa*).

7. Guided Visualization of Vishnu Sahasranama

Here is a simple **guided meditation** you can use before or after your chanting:

Close your eyes.
Inhale deeply...
Imagine yourself sitting by the banks of the Ganga. The air is cool, sacred.
You hear a conch (sankh) blow in the distance.
You are seated at the feet of Bhishma, who begins to chant.
As each name echoes, you see Lord Vishnu appearing in countless forms—
A protector, a healer, a child, a king, a friend.
His thousand names become a garland of light, encircling your body.
One by one, your worries melt.
One by one, your thoughts quiet.
There is only stillness...
Only the sound of the Divine...
Om Namo Bhagavate Vāsudevāya.

Practice this visualization for 5–10 minutes after your daily chant to **internalize the names as experience, not just recitation**.

8. Meditation While Listening (Shravana Dhyana)

For those who don't chant but love to listen, the Sahasranama can be experienced **through auditory immersion**.

How:

- Play a recorded chant (MS Subbulakshmi's version is widely loved)
- Sit comfortably, eyes closed, with a relaxed spine

- Focus all your attention on the **sound vibrations**
- Let the names **flow over you like a sacred stream**

This is a form of **shravanam**, one of the nine limbs of bhakti. Done daily, it builds **inner silence and steady devotion.**

9. Night Meditation with Sahasranama

Chanting or mentally reciting even a few names before bed is a gentle way to **cleanse the day and invoke peace**.

Practice:

- Light a lamp or candle.
- Sit at your altar or on your bed.
- Chant one verse, slowly and with feeling.
- Lie down with palms over the heart.
- Mentally repeat "Om Namo Narayanaya" until you fall asleep.

This practice not only improves sleep—it **infuses the subconscious** with divine presence.

10. Meditation for Children and Beginners

If you're new to meditation or introducing it to your children, keep it simple and joyful.

Ideas:

- Choose 1 name a day and draw it or color it.
- Chant 10 names before meals or bedtime.
- Use audio apps with repeat-and-respond formats.

- Ask: "What does this name mean to you?"

Meditation is not always silence—it's presence. Even a child chanting "Govinda" with joy is in meditation.

Chapter 10. Daily Chanting

Chanting the Vishnu Sahasranama (the Thousand Names of Lord Vishnu) daily is a deeply purifying and spiritually uplifting practice. The following is a traditional and practical guide for daily recitation:

1. Ideal Time for Chanting

- **Morning (Brahma Muhurta)** – Approximately 1.5 hours before sunrise (around 4:30 – 6:00 AM) is considered most auspicious.
- **Alternatively**, it can be chanted in the **evening** after sunset or before bedtime, preferably after a bath.

2. Preparation

- **Cleanliness**: Bathe and wear clean clothes. A calm, clean environment enhances concentration.

- **Altar or Image**: Sit before a picture or idol of Lord Vishnu, Krishna, or Narayana.
- **Posture**: Sit in a comfortable meditative posture (such as Padmasana or Sukhasana) facing east or north.

3. Mental Attitude

- **Devotion**: Begin with a pure heart and sincere devotion.
- **Focus**: Keep the mind focused on the Lord's form, qualities, and presence.
- **Silence or Soft Voice**: Chant audibly or mentally with clarity, not hurriedly.

4. Recitation Order (Optional but Traditional)

1. **Dhyanam** (Meditative Verses) – To invoke the presence of the Lord.
2. **Sankalpam** – A brief mental resolve to chant for a specific purpose (optional).
3. **Vishnu Sahasranama Stotram** – The full thousand names (starting from *Shuklam Bharadaram Vishnum...*).
4. **Phala Shruti** (Uttaranyasa verses) – The concluding verses (1–26), describing the benefits of chanting.
5. **Mangala Slokas** – Optional final prayers or personal prayers for blessings.

5. Frequency and Duration

- Daily recitation takes around **25–30 minutes**.
- Those unable to recite the full stotram daily may:

- Chant **selected verses** with devotion.
- Recite **one name with meaning** a day and meditate on it.
- Chant the **108 names** or the **main stanza (verse 24)** as a substitute.

6. Closing the Chanting

- Offer a prayer of gratitude.
- Perform **Namaskaram** (prostration or mental bowing).
- Pray for the well-being of all beings (Sarve Bhavantu Sukhinah).

7. Additional Tips

- Use a **Japa Mala** (rosary) if desired, but not mandatory.
- Maintain **regularity**—daily chanting builds discipline and spiritual momentum.
- Chanting with **family members** can enhance collective positivity.

Chapter 11. How to Memorize Vishnu Sahasranama

The *Sri Vishnu Sahasranama* is more than a chant—it's a spiritual discipline, a moving meditation, and a divine memory palace. To memorize it is to carry a portable temple in your heart and a sacred library in your mind.

While the idea of memorizing 1,000 names might seem daunting, with the right techniques, **devotion and consistency** can turn the impossible into a joy-filled journey. Many children in traditional Indian homes have memorized it before their teens. Many elders can recite it from heart well into their 80s. You can too.

This chapter provides a complete roadmap—based on **traditional methods, modern memory science, and devotional practice**—to help you learn and retain the Vishnu Sahasranama.

1. Why Memorize? The Inner Benefits

Before jumping into methods, it's important to know **why** memorizing the Sahasranama is so powerful:

- It transforms passive listening into **active remembrance** (*smarana*).
- It enhances **focus, concentration, and mental clarity**.
- It provides comfort, even when texts or devices aren't accessible.
- It makes **daily chanting effortless** and **deeply immersive**.
- Most importantly, it draws the Divine closer into your daily consciousness.

To memorize is to internalize—and once it's within you, **no one can take it away**.

2. Understand the Structure: Your First Key to Memory

The Sahasranama isn't just 1,000 random names—it's carefully structured.

Sections of the Vishnu Sahasranama:

1. **Invocation Verses (Dhyanam)** - 3 verses
2. **Main Sahasranama (1,000 Names)** - about 107 shlokas
3. **Phalashruti (Benefits)** - around 11 concluding verses

Rhythmic Meter

- Most verses follow the **Anushtup meter** (4 quarters per verse, 8 syllables per quarter).
- This rhythm helps the brain **chunk and recall information** better.

Memorizing by **verse**, not individual names, allows you to internalize **flow, meaning, and music**.

3. Set Realistic Milestones

The first rule of memorization: **Go slow to go far.**

Start with a pace that's manageable for your lifestyle:

Plan Type	**Target**	**Timeframe**
Basic	1 verse per day	~4 months
Moderate	2 verses per day	~2 months

Plan Type	Target	Timeframe
Accelerated	5–6 verses per day	~3 weeks

Don't rush. Instead, **repeat and reinforce**.

4. Listen Before You Learn

Before attempting to memorize, **immerse yourself in the sound**:

- **Listen daily** to a trusted recitation (MS Subbulakshmi's is a classic choice).
- Follow along with the text to build **aural familiarity**.
- Focus on **intonation, rhythm, and breaks** between verses.

Do this for at least 10–15 days before formal memorization. The brain will start forming **audio-visual linkages** automatically.

5. Use the "Repeat and Recall" Method

This is a traditional and effective technique used in Vedic learning.

How It Works:

1. **Repeat a single verse** 5–10 times while reading.
2. Then, **close the text** and attempt to recall it.
3. If you forget a line, peek, then repeat again.
4. Continue until the verse flows without looking.

Then move to the next verse—but **review yesterday's verse** before adding the new one.

This "build and review" method ensures long-term retention.

6. Break It Down: The "Chunking" Technique

Chunking is a memory technique used by linguists and memory athletes alike. In the Sahasranama, you can break down each verse into 2 or 4 chunks (based on syllables or logical meaning).

Example:

Verse:

Viśvaṁ viṣṇur vaṣaṭkāro bhūta-bhavya-bhavat-prabhuḥ

Bhūta-kṛd bhūta-bhṛd bhāvo bhūtātmā bhūta-bhāvanaḥ

Chunks:

- Viśvaṁ / Viṣṇur / Vaṣaṭkāro / Bhūta-bhavya-bhavat-prabhuḥ
- Bhūta-kṛd / Bhūta-bhṛd / Bhāvo / Bhūtātmā / Bhūta-bhāvanaḥ

By mastering small, meaningful groups, you reduce cognitive overload.

7. Use Visual Aids and Highlight Patterns

While you're using English transliteration, the brain still loves patterns.

Tips:

- **Highlight repeated prefixes** like "Bhūta-", "Viṣṇu-", or "Hari-".
- Use **colors** or **bold fonts** to mark similar sounds.
- Print the text in **chunked blocks** for easier visual digestion.

You may also write out verses by hand—this physical motion **reinforces memory**.

8. Recite With Movement or Mudra

The ancient Indian method of walking while reciting is called **Parayana Gati**.

- Walk slowly while repeating verses aloud.
- Swing arms gently with rhythm.
- This activates **motor memory + verbal memory + auditory memory**, tripling retention.

Alternatively, use a **japa mala** and touch one bead per verse to build tactile association.

9. Anchor Names with Meaning

Even if you don't study Sanskrit, **associating each name with an idea** creates strong memory hooks.

Examples:

- *Nārāyaṇa* – the one who rests on cosmic waters
- *Govinda* – protector of cows and beings
- *Acyuta* – the unchanging one

You don't need to understand every name—but occasionally pause and visualize or reflect on the name you just learned. This turns dry repetition into **devotional contemplation**.

10. Group Learning and Chant-Alongs

Learning with others builds accountability, fun, and rhythm.

- Join a **chanting group** at your local temple or online.
- Attend weekly **satsangs** where the Sahasranama is recited.

- Start a **"1 verse a day" challenge** with friends or family.

When chanted together, the vibration and flow make **learning faster and more joyful**.

11. Review, Revisit, Repeat

Here's the key to success: **spaced repetition**.

Sample Weekly Plan:

- **Day 1–5**: Learn 5 new verses.
- **Day 6**: Review all 5.
- **Day 7**: Recite the whole week's set **without looking**.

Every 3–4 weeks, do a **cumulative review**. The brain forgets what it doesn't revisit—so make review sacred.

12. Use Audio Tools and Technology

Today, we are blessed with tools our ancestors didn't have.

Use:

- **Recording apps**: Record yourself and play back
- **Flashcard apps**: (like Anki) to test verse recall
- **Looped audio tracks**: Play one verse on repeat until mastered
- **YouTube chant tutorials**: Follow with line-by-line visuals

Don't hesitate to blend **devotion and technology**—as long as the heart is in it, the method is valid.

13. Challenges and Encouragement

You will forget.
You will confuse lines.
You will get discouraged.

But remember: **this is not a performance. It is a prayer.** Even one verse learned with love carries **infinite merit**.

If you make a mistake, correct it gently. If you miss a day, restart without guilt. **Grace flows not from perfection, but from persistence.**

14. Milestone Rituals: Celebrate Progress

Make your journey joyful by marking milestones:

- After 10 verses: light a lamp and offer a prayer.
- After 50: chant before your family or deity.
- After 100: offer naivedyam (food) to Vishnu in thanks.

When you complete all 107 verses, you may choose to:

- Recite the **entire Sahasranama aloud on Ekadashi**.
- Teach it to someone else as an offering.
- Begin a second cycle for **deeper absorption**.

About The Author

Mrs. Payel Chakravarty is a writer at heart who beautifully blends technical precision with creative expression. Holding a **B.Tech and M.Tech in Information Technology**, along with a **certification from the Indian Institute of Management, Ahmedabad (IIMA)**, she brings both analytical depth and emotional insight to her work.

Based in India, Payel gracefully balances her roles as a mother of two, author, blogger, ghostwriter, freelancer, and homemaker. Writing has been her lifelong passion and spiritual refuge. Her work reflects her belief that words can heal, inspire, and transform lives.

Through her books, blogs, and online presence, she seeks to share stories and reflections that awaken inner peace and devotion in readers across the world.

You can connect with her and explore more of her work at:
Website:www.payelchakravarty.com
Email: contact@payelchakravarty.com

Note: If this book inspires YOU, and enhances your life in any way, it would be a dream come true to see your honest review on Amazon.

www.ingramcontent.com/pod-product-compliance
Ingram Content Group UK Ltd.
Pitfield, Milton Keynes, MK11 3LW, UK
UKHW021343190726
13845UKWH00027B/703

9 789334 303353